Lust for Power

LUST
FOR
POWER

BY

JOSEPH HAROUTUNIAN

WIPF & STOCK · Eugene, Oregon

Wipf and Stock Publishers
199 W 8th Ave, Suite 3
Eugene, OR 97401

Lust for Power
A Study of the Misuse of Power
By Haroutunian, Joseph
Copyright©1949 by Haroutunian, Joseph
ISBN 13: 978-1-60899-005-4
Publication date 5/1/2011
Previously published by C. Scribner's Sons, 1949

TO MY WIFE
WITH
LOVE AND GRATITUDE

Acknowledgments

The present writer is no exception to the rule that authors are debtors. Professor Louise P. Smith of Wellesley College, President R. Worth Frank of McCormick Theological Seminary, and Professor Herbert W. Schneider of Columbia University have contributed greatly to the making of this book. Without their encouragement and detailed criticisms this volume would have been larger and much poorer. Mr. William Savage of Charles Scribner's Sons has made his usual contribution as a competent and helpful publisher. Mrs. Glen Dilley and Mrs. Harold Davis have labored unsparingly in the typings of the manuscript. My wife, Helen, has influenced my work in a way which makes it her work as well as mine. To all these I extend my hearty thanks.

A book like this could not have been written without the labors of many a giant in the realm of thought. A reader interested in "sources" can find here a heritage which includes the works of Pascal, Thorstein Veblen, Karen Horney, Dostoevski, Herman Melville, Plato's Socrates and the writers of the Bible. Veblen and Melville provided the writer with the immediate impulse to write this book. They also dominated his mind repeatedly while at work. May all these be always remembered and studied!

JOSEPH HAROUTUNIAN

Contents

ACKNOWLEDGMENTS   vii

INTRODUCTION
Is There an Unnatural Use of Power?   1

CHAPTER I

NEW OCCASION FOR LUST
1. A New and Available Infinite   7
2. Life in the New Environment   12
3. A Taste of Absolute Power   14
4. Master and Slave: The New Spirit   16

CHAPTER II

LUST IN THE NEW SOCIETY
1. The New Dependence upon Men   24
2. Organized Power and the Common Man   26
3. The New Superiority   32
4. The New Inhumanity   35
5. Lust for Power   38

CHAPTER III

LUST IN THE MAKING
1. A Strange Disproportion   42
2. Of Lifetime: Persons and Things   47
3. Of Being, Having and Behaving   55
4. The Infinite and the Eternal   60

ix

5. The Origins of the Vices: Of Unreason   64
6. Power for Good and Goods for Power   72

CHAPTER IV

LUST FOR FREEDOM
1. The Peril in Prudence   77
2. Freedom as Arbitrary Will   81

CHAPTER V

GUILT IN THE CAREER OF LUST
1. The Bitterness in Lust   85
2. Guilt without God   87
3. Answers to Objections   91
4. The Mystery of Guilt   97
5. The New Innocence and Lust for Power   100

CHAPTER VI

MAN IN ISOLATION
A. The New Despair   104
1. The Soul of the Western Man   104
2. Behind the New Despair   108
3. Man without Neighbors   111
    a. The Philosopher   113
    b. The Romantic Poet   118
    c. The Layman   121
4. The Great Disappointment   123
    a. The Machine and the Void   123
    b. Irrelevant Science   126

CHAPTER VII

THE PROBLEM OF LOVE
1. A New Conspiracy of Silence   129
2. The Problem of Conversation: Of Isolation   130

3. The Congested World   132
4. Of Self-Pity, Self-Hatred, Pity, and Callousness   134
5. The Problem of Love   137

CHAPTER VIII

ANTIDOTE TO LUST

1. Love for Life   140
2. The Ambiguity of Existence   143
3. Civilisation and Culture   149
4. The Corruption of Culture   155
5. The Ambiguity of the Christian Faith   160
6. The Problem of Justice   165
7. Antidote to Lust   168

INDEX   173

Introduction:

OUR AGE HAS become obsessed with the problem of power. The enormous technological power in the western world, the recent misuses of it for wholesale destructions of men and property, the fear of future holocausts which are expected to "destroy western civilization," have made this problem the major concern of our time. Organized power everywhere has produced an anxiety which prevents a rational ordering of life for peace and welfare. In spite of all our efforts for a good use of our power, we live in an increasing fear of its ill use for universal ruin.

In political relations, and even in personal relations, our favorite way of dealing with other people's power is to match it with our own. We usually try to discourage others from dominating us with an impressive show of our own strength and our willingness to use it against them. Whenever groups with opposed interests confront one another, such a procedure is inevitable. Even in the most peaceful of societies, a balance of power is necessary for justice and freedom. The absence of such a balance in any set of human relations presents an irresistible temptation for the strong to tyrannize over the weak. In a good society, power is controlled with power, through persuasion if possible, through open conflict if necessary.

No discerning observer can deny the effectiveness of this traditional way of dealing with power. It must, however, be admitted that in our day, all balance of power is precarious. Power today is too great and too inebriating. There is no one to distribute it in such a way that there shall be a stable bal-

1

ance of it among nations, races, classes and regions. The historic ways of dealing with it through "power politics" and open warfare have become much too perilous. It is no longer intelligent and enough to match power with power and to expect even a reasonable measure of security and peace. We need a new understanding of power as it affects the human soul; a new insight into the inner dynamics of the heart of man where power becomes a source of lust which denatures him and finally destroys him.

Our conception of the works of power in us has been simple in the extreme. Even while we are aware of the corrupting influences of power in others, we have lacked aptitude for discovering the same influences in ourselves and for making a fruitful study of them for our common health and welfare. The usual assumption about power is that men and nations seek after it for their security. We take it for granted that power is essential for survival and the good life. Therefore, we want it and want more of it. A simple, obvious, natural desire for life and good is supposed to explain the many-sided conflicts of our time. Why are there so many and protracted conflicts between race and race, creed and creed, class and class, nation and nation, yea even continent and continent? Why is there a ubiquitous bid for power in every conceivable grouping of men: in "city halls," shops, schools, churches, and even families? Because all men want to be secure and to live a happy life.

No doubt, in a time like ours the passion for security is intense. And so is the desire for enjoying a maximum of goods. But we must not overlook men's universal impulse to have their way. People want security and prosperity, and they also want freedom. No doubt they want freedom for the sake of goods and security in the enjoyment of them. But they want it also for its own sake. It is not enough to be secure with one's goods; one must also be free to do with them as one will. Liberty of action is essential to one's pleasure with life and goods. Men have been known to jeopardize both life and goods for the sake of liberty. There are many times when nothing is so gratifying as to do what one will simply because one has willed to do it. It is important to keep such "irrationality" in mind when we consider the will to power.

Sheer liberty of action is the sign of another and perhaps greater good: power over our fellowmen. To lord it over others is a means of security, freedom, riches, status, etc. But also, it is a good in itself; a good which can overwhelm every other good dictated by reason and conscience alike. It is strangely gratifying to make people come and go at our bidding, to over-rule their minds and their wills, to take away their power and thus virtually to annihilate them. There is an "irrational" but nonetheless soul-filling self-fulfilment in mastery over human beings. There is no pleasure quite like it; and for its sake, men have risked every good and done every conceivable evil. It is well to remember these facts and to take them seriously.

Now, this "lust for power" is irrational and wicked. It must not be mentioned in polite discourse, whether political or scientific. Nevertheless, the unmentionable thing is there. Every man knows that his enemies, those unreasonable and vicious people, have a good dose of it in their souls. There is no other way of explaining their stupid and settled resistance to the common good. Hence, to say the least, some people are possessed of a lust for power. It is not prudent to say it publicly, but in truth a great many people, perhaps most people, love power for its own sake. This may even be true of one-self, but of course, a little, very, very little.

The universality of lust for power has led to the tradi-tional and prevalent doctrine that this lust is "natural." His-torians, philosophers and scientists alike have worked with the assumption that lust for power is an automatic expression of "human nature." Even men like Hobbes, Pascal, Spinoza, Bertrand Russell, Lord Acton, Thorstein Veblen, and Jacob Burkhardt, who have been aware of the corrupting influence of power, have treated the "will to power" as a natural human impulse. Nietzsche went so far as to elevate it to the status of a cosmic principle, and found it in wind and fire as well as in plants, animals and men. Any illuminating and helpful distinction between a natural and unnatural impulse for power, which is basic for the following study, is, so far as the writer knows, absent from our literature on the subject.

Hence it is a common practice among reasonable men to seek to mitigate this "natural" lust with appeals to the common good. When journalists unload their "facts" upon us and analysts explain them for us, when negotiators come together and wise men seek to compromise and cooperate, they all assume that the will to live has no formidable enemy except ignorance. They hope that, given sufficient knowledge and good sense, men and nations in conflict will not allow their pursuit of power to plunge them into ruin. It seems to them altogether natural and reasonable that men and nations should prefer life and good to the love of power. What chance has a natural impulse for power against an equally natural impulse for life and happiness?

But, lust for power is not natural. It is essentially different from that natural love of power whose end is the natural and rational good of man. Lust for power is a corruption of nature and it has nothing but contempt for reason and its quest for a happy life. The chief end of lust is its own gratification and lust for power is the pursuit of power as its own absolute end. Hence it is both absurd and futile to meet lust for power with counsels of prudence. This lust is not in the service of good, and no prospect of good will persuade it to turn aside from its career of vice and villainy. It is disastrous to treat lust for power as a natural impulse and to try to discipline it with reason or force. A new understanding of the genesis of this lust in the human soul has now become indispensable.

Moralists attribute lust for power to pride, ambition, greed, etc. Indeed, these vices lead to lust. But they do not explain its origin, since they themselves include lust and grow out of it. There is no man who is proud or ambitious or greedy, who lacks a strong impulse to lord it over others; and it is impossible to say which comes first, his vice or his lust. The "moral" explanations of lust get us nowhere. They give us forms of lust and not its cause or causes.

Nowadays, lust is often regarded as a disease due to insecurity, anxiety, and frustration. Here, we have in fact gone a step further. These maladies of the mind produce inner turmoils in which lust for power is born and becomes virulent. We are deeply indebted to the psychologists who have uncovered such sources of lust and, what is more illuminating, have given us the insight that symptom and cause in human behavior do not always coincide. We have thus moved beyond the common assumption that lust for power is either simply natural or simply wicked.

However, we must face the further question as to the origins of "the neurotic personality." Some psychologists have taken the position that neuroticism is due to the suppression of natural impulses, especially of the sex impulse. This suppression makes for a repository of unconscious drives which are at war with conscious life. Such warfare is at the root of anxiety, frustration, aggression, and the rest. When the inner schism is removed, men are reintegrated and restored to natural health. . . .

Other psychologists emphasize the social factors which make for mental disease. A society in which men live in constant fear of their jobs and goods is a hotbed of anxiety. One in which men are repeatedly frustrated in their pursuit of happiness is a jungle of frictions. Exploitation, segregation, defamation, make for resentment and lust for power. Glaring inequalities, contradictions between ideal and practice, the sense of guilt, etc., turn people into neurotics, who are men haters and lovers of power for its own sake.

Such explanations of lust for power are undeniably valid. They are necessary for understanding its emergence in a given instance and setting. Nevertheless, the appearance of lust for power in *any* setting requires a different explanation from the ones given by the "psychologist." If this lust is due to neuroticism, then there are innumerable neurotics who are not even expected to consult the psychologist. These are the "well adjusted" people, the sane and sensible folk who constitute the healthy majority. They are to be found most frequently among the leaders of the people, among men in high places who contribute a disproportionate share to the good and evil in the world. In short, lust for power is not limited to neurotics according to any reasonably exclusive definition. It is not enough to say that nearly everybody is a neurotic. If neuroticism making for lust for power appears under the best of social conditions, it takes more than social conditions to explain it.

There is in man a frustration which neither long life nor "many goods" can overcome and remove. There is an anxiety which persists no matter how well a man is insured against misfortune and loss. The *malaise* of the human soul is occasioned by vicissitudes of life; but it is not caused or produced by them.

Man is not satisfied with a long life, and he is not satisfied with goods. What then will satisfy him? *Nothing* will satisfy him. Nothing can become a substitute for the good without which no good is good enough. And this good is none other than a man's existence which is good in a unique and primary sense. But this good shall be lost. We anticipate this loss necessarily and live under its shadow throughout our lives. This shadow is cast upon the whole of human existence and alters the face of everything. In it the love of power for good is transformed into lust for power, for itself and for evil. The purpose of this book is to examine this transformation and thus to open the way for a more authentic knowledge of man and his ways.

CHAPTER I

New Occasion for Lust

1. A NEW AND AVAILABLE INFINITE

LUST FOR POWER, like pride and contempt, is an aristocratic vice. It reminds one of Milton's Satanic Majesty who hurled defiance at the Creator of the universe; of Adolf Hitler who aspired to rule the world; of conquerors, kings and captains of industry, labor leaders, millionaires, bishops and bureaucrats. Almost all bosses are contaminated with it; so are one's rivals and superiors. One sometimes suspects its presence among one's neighbors and friends, and even in the members of one's own family.

However, among equals or nearly equals, lust for power usually lacks that obtrusive energy which calls for corresponding action. It is better to ignore it and to forget about it. One must watch the men of power, and see to it that they do not turn into tyrants. But it is unnecessary, in bad taste, and even harmful, to be concerned with lust for power among the "common people," who, like oneself, care next to nothing about lording it over their fellowmen.

The "common man," this teacher or that shopkeeper, is not aware of an inordinate ambition for power. He has little hope of "getting to the top," and would not even profess a desire for it. All he wants is a steady job, a decent house in a good neighborhood, enough food, drink, and clothing; a car, three radios, a refrigerator, a gas range; enough money for movies, magazines, dinners out and other moderate fun; enough to send his children to a good school or college, enough for insurance and other bills, enough so that he does not have to worry or count his pennies every time he wants to buy something. He does not care much for "power." All he wants is to live like a decent, civilized human being according to American standards.

For the "common man" it is goods and not power that make for a good life. There is much he can have. He wants the freedom and opportunity to go after it. He wants to have friends and influence people. He wants to associate with the right people, at home, at the golf course, at the club or at church. He wants to get along. All this he wants so that he may have more goods and enjoy them among his fellowmen. It is the commonplace judgment of our time that the good life consists in the possession and enjoyment of goods; and that the more the goods, the better the life. Hence, the most effective characteristic of the common man today is a permanent will to multiply and improve his goods. Everybody assumes it is both natural and reasonable to want more money and to buy more goods.

There is of course nothing new about the desire for possessions. Men have always preferred being rich to being poor. Their women have always preferred a silk dress to one made of cotton or wool, and costly perfumes to cold water. For the sake of sweets and soft couches, men have broken every law of justice and peace. They have exploited and oppressed, and done everything from lying to murder, so that they might eat, and drink, and be merry, above their fellowmen.

However, the common wealth of pre-industrial societies imposed strict limitations upon the common man's appetite for goods. Living in an "economy of scarcity," men had to be content with a frugal diet and few goods. A man, most men, could have had so much and no more. All things were limited. Foods had to be eaten in season and as produced nearby. Woven material came from looms operated with human hands and feet, and there was a limit as to how much could be produced in this fashion. Woodwork and ironwork were done with tools attached to the limited physical powers of the artisan. And bookbinders and silversmiths worked end-lessly to produce the few specimens of their handiwork. Goods were limited, money was limited, and possibilities of enjoy-ment were limited. There was a limit to everything, and there was a corresponding limit, or at least discouragement, to want-ing things.

The indefinite productivity of our machines has given us a new appetite for possessions. There are an astronomical number and variety of goods available. We have billions of competent and tireless slaves which can make anything we want and in any amount we want it. The contents of the average household in an "industrial society" are breathtaking as compared with those in a house in a "backward country." From the cellar to the attic, the place is full of things: furni-ture, furnishings, and things to wear; hardware, glassware, chinaware, and silver; toys, books, magazines, and records; canned and packaged and bottled goods, soaps, drugs and sundry other "preparations"; tools and gadgets for every conceivable purpose; and then, radios in every other room, the vacuum cleaner with attachments, the gas stove, the re-frigerator, the incredible washing machine, the sewing ma-chine, and the car in the garage. Not everyone has all this. But every one might have it, and more; everyone wants it, and more. One has only to listen to the radio, or read a magazine, or merely walk down the street, to meet more than one thing too helpful or too enjoyable to be missed. The newly discovered advertising genius of the race will see to it that we shall at all times want any number of things we do not now possess.

When quantity loses its lure, quality comes in with its colorings of infinity. The grades of goods produced by the machines permit of indefinite improvement. There are more expensive foods to eat and better cut clothes to wear. There are radios which make better pieces of furniture and produce purer sounds. There are more beautiful cars which go faster, drive more smoothly, and are more roomy and comfortable.

One could have a better house in a better section of town. One could have a fine house by the sea and another in the mountains. And one could always improve the furnishings of each house. There are better restaurants and better seats in the shows; and one could go out more often. One could join a better club, go to a better church, play on a better golf course and have better friends. One could develop one's esthetic sensibilities indefinitely and collect beautiful objects and always find new ones more expensive and beautiful.

There is always more and more which lures men on without end. The hope of "the progress of mankind upwards and onwards forever," is not a mere product of undisciplined fancy. It is a reasonable response to the unlimited possibilities of multiplication in a society dominated by machines. Our "power machines" are tireless and prodigious producers. Their powers and numbers are always on the increase. They can concentrate their forces and do the impossible. Their skill and efficiency are absolutely superior to any skill any man or beast could achieve. They can always be multiplied and improved, and replaced by better machines which will produce more and better things at less cost in time and energy. The machines will always progress; so will the goods they produce, in quality and quantity; so will civilization progress and culture also with it. The health of body and mind will improve. Morals and manners will improve. Knowledge will improve and truth will increase. There will be more light, and mankind will progress upwards and onwards forever.

A machine civilization has turned the spirits of men towards a new and numerical infinity. The limits which nature imposed upon human life are removed. Civilizations based upon man's finitude and the cultures they produced have become outmoded. In the old world, men sought a "good" which transcended nature and always eluded them. In the new world, men seeks well defined goods which are attainable and virtually innumerable. Before, men conceived of the good in relation to their misery in "nature"; and they sought a life beyond it. In one manner or another, they were concerned with life beyond the reach of death, or "eternal life." Today, the troubles of men only inspire them to redouble their efforts towards multiplying their goods and securing the condition of enjoying them. The new answer of man to evil is "the economy of abundance." A new infinite has replaced the old eternal.

Goods, unlike the "good" of the old philosophers, are no undefined and unattainable quiddity. They have colors, and shapes, and uses, and they are everywhere. There are no gods which place them beyond our reach. We do not need to qualify our cupidity with moderation or apathy. We need not say, "sour grapes," and turn our minds and hearts to some "higher good." We need not teach ourselves to prefer virtue and piety which shall make us contented in our want. In short, we need not confuse our acquisitive impulses with others which shall blunt the edge of our frustrations. Hence, the will to have can now operate with an unhampered energy. We may now turn from a doubtful destiny in nature to the prospects of a eutopia of our own making. We can now pursue an infinity of goods without the hesitations and the humiliations which attended the worship of the gods and the pursuit of "eternal life." We can now be singleminded, "scientific," confident, consistent, and persistent, in the exercise of our energies towards an "abundant life." It may be that such a love of having, as found among men with machines, is a part of "human nature." Nevertheless, as informed by the new infinite, it acts as a new impulse and produces new effects.

One commonplace illustration will have to suffice. The love of comfort is unlimited among us. Men have always loved comfort, but men with machines love it with a new passion. Think of the comforts of house and furniture! Think of the ease induced by the telephone, the car, the electric lights, and the frigidaire and the washing machine. Think of the human energy saved by our thousand machines and gadgets! It is inevitable that under the circumstances, the love of ease and comfort should become a predominant human passion. A salesman can sell anything if he can show that it is easy to use. "No trouble at all. Just push this, and turn that, and there she goes." "Get this car, and you won't know you're driving it." "Look at this radio. Push one button, and it is on and at the right station." Ah, the radio! Stay home, put on your slippers, pick up the paper, and listen to music, drama, sketch, news, mystery, comedy, harangue, comments, in any order whatever, and interspersed with apostrophes to soap, oil, cereal, vitamins, cigarettes, wines, and steel. Just sit down and listen while you doze. There is nothing on the radio you cannot understand with half a brain. The same is true of the movies, "best-sellers," sermons, and lectures. Everything is easy and will become easier as we progress. Happiness is inversely proportionate to activity. Upholstered chairs, soft and pliant against the bottom and the back, are ubiquitous symbols of the cult of ease and comfort. Here is an authentic cult, inspired by the machines, promoted by business, and followed by every sensible man in our society.

2. LIFE IN THE NEW ENVIRONMENT

The man living in dependence upon the sun and the soil exists circumscribed and limited at every turn. If the sun does not shine propitiously, his crops do not yield fruit. There is nothing he can do about it. He lives under a constant contradiction between his desire for happiness and the ways of nature. He can have so much, and at given times. He must be ready to suffer discomfort, disease, and even death. He is at the mercy of nature and its gods, and he knows it.

The precariousness of man's existence in nature has frequently dampened his enthusiasm for it, and made him somewhat of a rebel. Life was perennially ambiguous. With one hand "Nature" blessed man, with the other it cursed him. Hence, his gratitude "for all the blessings of this life" was colored with a fearful fury and muttered resentment. He was not altogether at home in nature. There was a constant tension between himself and its gods. His civilization gave him power over nature, and his culture gave him freedom from it. He cultivated magic and science on the one hand, and art and wisdom on the other. Thus the rigors of nature were to the soul as rain is to a plant. They gave it strength and enabled it to grow into a beflowered and fruitful tree.

The life of man today is precarious in its own way, generally and extremely precarious. However, the new environment is man-made, constructed with machinery under his absolute control. Man is sovereign in his new habitat, and there is no felt tension between him and the machine powers around him. Everything is for his use, and the use he makes of it depends upon his skill and ingenuity. All machines, as machines, are essentially simple and transparent. Provided a man knows their construction, he can operate them at will. Machines do not indulge in the unpredictable resistances of "God's creatures." They do not vary their humors and performances as do the beasts. They are not independent and changeable as the weather. Hence, the difficulties between men and machines are mere peccadillos. Man is in essential harmony with his new environment.

The story of civilization is the story of man's growing freedom and sovereignty in nature. But such sovereignty has also been bondage. Nature has shaped man's ideals and motives even while it has yielded to his ingenuity. The more power man has had over his world, the more "worldly" he has become. His imagination which subdued nature has also been subdued by it. His reason has provided him with the means for attaining ends dictated by the environment. His desires have been attached to these ends and his will has yielded to them. Man the lord of nature has been lorded over by nature. But man has continually rebelled against his subjection, and this rebellion has generated culture.

Man's power over the machine which is the work of his own hands is perfect. He can make virtually every machine, tool and gadget for every purpose inspired by machine, tool and gadget. Every time he wants to satisfy a need made by machines, he can turn to a machine and exhaust both purpose and will in the use of it. Such a man assimilates the machine; but also, he is assimilated by it.

Man loves the machine with a love which he never gave the gods of nature. The latter were niggardly and unreliable, whereas the machine is a veritable Santa Claus who shows up every day with bags always full and apparently inexhaustible. The machine is the new god, "infinite, eternal, unchangeable," the giver of every good and perfect gift, the lord of "the economy of abundance," more generous than any god that ever walked the earth. The love of this god is most just and the service of it is perfect freedom. And this service is the new bondage. Freedom in nature was a "pushover" as compared to freedom in our machine-made environment.

3. *A TASTE OF ABSOLUTE POWER*

The machines which make everything are the perfect slaves. They have no private life. They hide no secrets from their makers. They have no will against the will of their makers. Even the ass has his moods and his own rhythm of life: there is no telling when he will pull back and refuse to go. But not so with the machine. Once a machine is put together rightly, filled with the right fuel and lubricated with the right grease, all one has to do is to turn it on. You pick up the phone and speak to anyone you please. When you are finished, you put it down and walk away. When you come back, it will be there as you left it and ready to repeat. The car is where you left it and waiting for you. The refrigerator and the water heater keep going, untired, uncomplaining, and absolutely passive. You can go on, week after week, month after month, turning on and turning off, and your machines will heat for you, cool for you, cut for you, clean for you, speak, write, and sing for you. They will feed you, clothe you, and carry you around. They will give you what you want and do anything you want, as you want it, and as long as you want. If you do not want it, all you have to do is to shut the blame thing off. You are the master, and taste daily of absolute or unresisted power.

When a man can have his way in one set of relations, it goes against the grain not to have it in others. If the machine is an abject slave, why not "nature"? Why should a man not plant and pull out as he will? Why should he not disembowel the earth, cut down the trees, cage and cross the animals, as he will? Thanks to his science and ingenuity with machines, he has a new mastery upon nature. And what can keep him from exercising it? His power over nature is only a little less than his power over his machines, and in both instances it is informed with the same will to have his way. Railroads, bridges, canals, dams, tunnels, projects for removing mountains and filling up valleys, for turning forests into fields and deserts into fertile lands, for changing the face of the earth according to the desire and taste of man—what are all these but mastery established and extended until hardly anything can stand in the way of man?

With such mastery over their environment, men are not loath to master also their fellowmen. The man with the machine hates resistence from any quarter. He cannot abide opposition to his will and is unhappy until his will is unopposed. Neither friend nor relative nor partner must stand in his way. No man or group of men must interfere with his pursuit of goods and his enjoyment of them. The government must help him and not block him. The school must teach him how to get ahead and not confuse his mind with useless knowledge. His membership in the club must serve him well, and the church to which he goes and contributes must pay dividends in improved opportunities for an abundant life. No race or color must stand in his way. No nation must challenge his way of doing things. No class or creed must be allowed to overrule his will and impede the progress of civilization. When any man or group of men will not let him have his way that is, when they challenge his freedom, they must by all means be incapacitated. He is a free man, and will rather die than give up his freedom. And he will more readily kill for it.

4. *MASTER AND SLAVE: THE NEW SPIRIT*

Man's relation to his machines is ambiguous. As a thing, the machine is a lifeless and will-less thing, utterly knowable and completely in the power of its maker. On the other hand, the machine as experienced, is shot through with ideas and images which subsist as components of the living mind. A man's mind is himself engaged in thought. The contents of his mind are what *he* imagines, lives, and hopes with. They arouse his passions, motivate his will and condition his acts. Hence, images of machines and machine made goods take possession of the mind and qualify a man's total existence. The radio as experienced is far from passive as a mere thing. It affects me with the collective power of all the sounds that have come out of it. I see it or imagine it with memories of my favorite programs. It means to me news every hour on the hour, sports broadcasts, political speeches, and hours of excellent music. I hate to be without my radio for very long. When something goes wrong with it, I call the repair man immediately. When it is fixed, I turn it on again, and anyone can see that I am happy and satisfied. The car is not merely a car. It means driving my children to school. It means a pleasant summer in the country. It means entertaining, and being entertained, going places and seeing things, and unlimited opportunities for pleasure. The vacuum cleaner means clean floors throughout the house. The sewing machine means pretty dresses for our daughter. The gas range means good food, and the frigidaire means a tasty bite and a cold drink. And who shall count the the meanings of the electric lights?

The machines define the good and regulate our existence. They do not resist us, and we cannot resist them. They make us free and they bind us to themselves. They possess us as we possess them. They confuse us, tempt us, and at last over-throw us.

The sheer passivity of the machine must not blind us to its irresistible power over the spirit of man. Man can do any-thing he will with his machines. But also, the goods and powers provided by his machines bring about a complete re-orientation in his existence. In his intercourse with machines and machine-made goods, he becomes possessed of a new spirit which masters him and makes him to serve the machines as the source of all true and palpable good.

The spirit evoked by the machine is a living power op-posed to our existence as persons. It tempts us to turn away from our perennial concerns with duty and destiny. It per-suades us to quench our compassions with our fellowmen and to dissociate power from justice and integrity. It teaches us to ignore death and to bid farewell to the quest for wisdom. It will promise anything and everything: perfect health, perfect power, unmixed enjoyments, endless happiness—if men will only forget to be "people." It is a most subtle spirit. To the good it will promise good and to the evil it will promise evil. When it gets through with men, they can no longer tell good from evil, or light from darkness.

The machine is the source of the good life as we have come to conceive it. Hence we are attached to it almost as strongly as we are to life itself. The people used to the Amer-ican or civilized way of life are so bound to the machine that they would suffer unbearable physical and mental dis-comfort without it. Hence they are attached to the machine with an extreme tenacity, all the stronger because it is un-conscious. Whatever their contemplative ideals, in existence they hold on to the machines and the goods provided by them. Good becomes evil and evil becomes good as they contribute or fail to contribute to the good as defined and made avail-able by the machines. Nobody and nothing can stand per-sistently in the way of goods without being set aside as evil. Families are broken, friends alienated, communities embittered and nations turned into enemies for the sake of machine power and machine made goods. Men are willing to risk even death and destruction for the sake of the good life as made by the machine. Incredible as it may be, goods are preferred to life. And all this bespeaks a most desperate bondage.

The new spirit is both like and unlike the spirits or demons which harassed our superstitious ancestors. There is the initial suspicious looking fact that since the arrival of the machine, the older spirits have disappeared in shame and confusion. These good-for-nothings, whom men used to petition for health and goods, are ousted and replaced by the spirit inspired by the machine. The latter has delivered men from bondage to the old time spirits and established itself in their place, only with more power.

Like the old spirits, the new spirit thrives on its ambiguous relation to man. To objectify it is superstitious, but to deny it objectivity is to be blind to its confirmed power. It is a modification and corruption of the human spirit, hence it is subjective rather than objective. But it takes possession of men and reduces them to a bondage which is all the more hopeless because it is camouflaged as spontaneity and freedom. Hence it is objective to the will if not to the mind. The new spirit, like the old, is abysmally clever in convincing men alternately of their freedom and unfreedom. In this way, men become possessed of deep contradictory convictions and in the ensuing confusion they are subjected to a bondage which is as real as it is ambiguous. They are given to alternate moods of omnipotence and impotence which cancel each other and leave them with a void. In this void, the new spirit is lord, building up and tearing down without rhyme or reason. In our age, when the power of the spirits is all but denied, the doings of the new spirit are all the more maddening and ruinous. Hence a debilitating anxiety, like that of those possessed of spirits, is a universal fact among people emancipated by the machine.

The older and dethroned spirits promised much but gave

little. Gods frequently failed to fructify the womb or to send down rain as needed. The new spirit is much more dependable. When you work with it, you can cure disease, fill your house with goods and live in secure opulence. It is a wonder-working god which deserves men's faith and the service they render it. But now, as in the old days, there is a deception. The promise and the gift do not coincide. Goods are delivered, but the good is withheld; which is readily proved by the fact that goods must be increased indefinitely with the hope that the good will thereby be attained. The old spirits deceived by failure to deliver the goods, the new deceives by failure to deliver the good. And of the two deceptions the latter is the greater.

The malefaction of the new spirit goes even deeper. It tempts men to be at once fascinated and repelled by the good. It tempts men to pursue goods, and in doing so, to fear the good. The good is in "justice, mercy and peace." It is in consistency and integrity, in living according to truth and right. It inheres in men and not in things. It is other than the goodness of goods and without it goods are not good. But the machine-made spirit teaches otherwise. It identifies the good with goods and induces men to dread it except as thus identified. It persuades men that there is no good other than goods. Thus men come to dread good as evil and to love evil as good. Thus it is that an apparent good produces evil as sparks fly upward. Henceforth all is confusion. The possessed yearn for good and perpetrate evil. They seek life and cultivate death. They grasp for power and freedom, and are reduced to the impotence of bondage. The new spirit makes for self-contradiction; self-contradiction makes for unreason; and unreason is the death of man.

The new spirit is a monstrosity born of a union of incompatibles; of the spirit of man and the power of machines. Men and machines belong to two radically different orders of being. Man is an organism, the machines are organized or put together. A man grows, a machine remains as it is made. A man struggles for maintaining his existence and lives anticipating his death. A machine neither struggles nor exists anticipating its end. A man loves himself, a machine loves neither itself nor anything else. A man lives in a community, sharing the passions of other men. The machine exists in an aggregation and in sheer indifference to other machines. When a man dies, other men are grieved. When a machine breaks down, it is replaced and all goes on as before. A man imagines, hopes and becomes anxious. The machine is free from such perturbations. Man pursues a destiny he does not attain and an integrity he does not achieve. The machine cares for neither duty nor destiny. Man is a person, the machine is a thing.

The new spirit is a miracle of misbegottenness. It is a corruption, a degeneration of both men and machines, a turning of two goods into an evil. It is a transformation of power into bondage, of grace in both men and machines into a deformity. However, the primary source of this perversion is man and not the machine.

Power in our society is essentially impersonal. It is rooted in financial credit, raw materials, power machines, machine tools, machines for everything from manufacture to sale. It is in the hands of men who are above all bankers, directors, technicians, workers, distributors, salesmen, etc. Men and things together constitute concatenations which subsist by systems of impersonal power. Even the intelligence and will involved in these systems partake of the impersonality of the latter, both in operation and in end. Money, men and machines alike are subordinate to the system in which they exist and subsist. Power in such a system is least contaminated by considerations of humanity. Being neither personal, nor animal, nor vegetable, it discourages sentiments of kinship among men and of piety towards their environment. Hence, the pursuit of power in modern life is singularly free from the distractions of conscience and humanity. And this freedom makes for a new barbarism.

The theory that social conflict is a leftover is not without reason. Business with machine made goods requires a settled, orderly, and peaceful society. There must be stability in money and prices. One must be able to depend upon an established difference between cost and value. One must be able to count on a steady sale of commodities and a steady accumulation of profit. One must be able to enjoy security in the use of profit made. Moreover, the machine process itself demands steady application and improvement. Hence, in an industrial society peace and order are indispensable. Where profit is *via* commerce rather than by conquest, the bias against violent change is very strong.

However, social conflict is not inversely proportionate to industrial development. On the contrary, the more complex and highly organized the industry, the more deadly the conflicts in a given society. The most perilous oppositions today are initiated by groups with the greatest amount of machine power at their disposal. And the chief reason for this apparent stupidity, this apparent cultural lag, is that the profit-motive is now subordinate to the power-motive, and the "instinct of workmanship" is subordinate to both. Those who control the machines seek at once profit and power. Profit they share with the shareholders, but power remains in their hands. And power is a good in itself as well as the source of all goods. The greater the power, the greater good it is, and the more it is used for its own sake. Men engaged in group conflicts today sacrifice goods, peace, and even technological progress, for the sake of power. They accept every manner of social evil, they risk the social order itself, rather than part with power. Any calculus of prosperity and pleasure would dictate cooperation. But such a calculus calculates little of the social dynamics of our time. It leaves out the impulse for power which has acquired a new potency among us.

The notion that a capitalism infatuated with the profit-motive is the primary cultural anachronism of our time is largely misleading. Such capitalism today is an ideology rather than a formative fact. It is being replaced steadily by another capitalism in which not property but power dominates the ambitions and actions of men. The great men whose pictures appear in the business sections of big city papers are presidents, vice-presidents, directors, executives, managers, and the like, and not those of investors or owners of capital. The latter appear, if anywhere, in the society columns. It is the men of power as men of power and not owners of property as owners of property who have the lion's share in the control of our economic life. These do not compete for profit; they eliminate competition for the sake of power. They produce and withhold production, they sell and refuse to sell, with a confused intention of holding on to and increasing their power. They seek to concentrate power rather than diffuse prosperity. The power of the machines and not the profit of the investors is the chief end of their work. This new thing may be capitalism, but it certainly is not the traditional article. It is not a lag but a perilous thrust for power.

Communism operates similarly. The difference between the new capitalism and communism is the difference in the *loci* of power in the two "systems." Under capitalism, machine power is in the hands of "industrialists." Under communism, it is in the hands of "politicians." The conflict between them is centered in the issue of control over the machine power in a given society. The rest, the complicated and confusing rest, is secondary, and by no means explains the virulence of the struggle between them. Whether in capitalism or in communism, we are confronted with the same straight bid for power which is new and deadly for the whole world. It is fatal to think of capitalism as a dying order, or of communism as the hope of the future. Both are informed with a new impulse for power which is also a new state of bondage. Unless this impulse is radically qualified, the world will see little of peace or common welfare.

The real contours of the mechanism of power in the western world are concealed by rich drapings of approved tradition. Even in fascism, the love of order, discipline, self-subordination, self-sacrifice for the good of the nation, visions of peace and plenty, etc., made the new power palatable to those who submitted to it. The impulse for the new power in communism is confused by visions of an economy of abundance for the greatest happiness of the greatest number, not excluding any race, tongue, or people. The same in the new capitalism is confused by the passion for liberty, property, equality of opportunity, the Four Freedoms and political democracy. The new power would be at a great disadvantage were it not so nobly justified by our culture, which gives it free course by concealing its true character and supremacy. Our cultural heritage, our humanitarian impulses and moral ideals, impede our understanding of the new power and incapacitate us against it. In such confusion, together with the obvious and fascinating benefits of this power, criticism becomes fatuous and almost futile. There is much talk of "liberty, equality, fraternity," while the new power brings us closer and closer to the brink of ruin. Apparently there is enough "idealism" to cover up the biggest bid for power; and yet power has its way with men and ideals alike.

CHAPTER II

Lust in the New Society

1. *THE NEW DEPENDENCE UPON MEN*

DEPENDENCE UPON the machines is also dependence upon men. It is upon men that we depend for the goods without which we cannot exist. Men make the machines and control them. Men's absolute dependence upon nature is replaced by a new absolute dependence upon men. It is now as perilous to offend some men as it was to offend some god. It is now men and not gods who can deprive a man of the water he drinks and the food he eats. In all things good and evil, we are dependent upon men and not upon nature or its gods. We live in a man made world, a world run by men, and in it we either live or perish. Every man, no matter how he struts and protests, fears his fellowmen above all else.

Dependence upon nature, and receiving good and evil from her, call for resignation to fate. Dependence upon the machine is disguised as mastery and calls only for skillful manipulation. But dependence upon men, being neither fatal nor lordly, is an invitation to the pursuit of power and superiority. Nature is irresistible. The machine need not be resisted. But man is resistible and will be resisted, lest he nullify one's will or, which is the same, violate one's person. One's very dependence upon others makes power indispensable. Thus human intercourse is an occasion for grasping after power. And when human relations involve complete dependence upon others, as is the case in our society, the pursuit of power becomes a primary and persistent preoccupation. No man is happy unless there is someone he dominates.

Such lording is lacking in that detached ingenuity with which we treat inanimate objects. It is a response to men who intend their deeds and choose to do evil where they might have done good. If men were more humane, there would be less need for anxiety about power. We could then live in peace and relax for the enjoyment of our goods. But men will not have it that way. They love to "show off" their power and to lord it over their fellowmen. Thus they do wrong and incur guilt. Everybody knows it is wrong to lord it over people and that it is humiliating to be lorded over by others. Hence the lords expect resentment and ill will; and the slaves, especially in a "free society," are seldom free from the malice expected of them. The masters treat their underlings with condescension and contempt; and the latter reciprocate with obeisance which is at once obsequious and hateful. The lords are lords in peril. The slaves are eager to throw off their bonds. Lord and lorded over alike are possessed of a constant impulse for power. Thus an absolute impulse for power works in the strong and weak alike; and this impulse, being directed towards human beings, is seldom free from bitterness which turns the love of power into a lust. In our society, with its gigantic powers, both the love of domination and the bitterness in it are indefinitely energized. The powerful have too much to lose and the weak have too much to gain. There is much power for many people. Hence, in our midst, the love of power is as persistent as it is widespread. And since power sought or possessed is power over men, the love of it is mixed with effective doses of envy, contempt, resentment, ill will, etc., which embitter life at its very roots and turn it into a thing without joy.

The bitterness in the impulse for power is due also to a radical disappointment with one's fellowmen. In our "acquisitive society," the pursuit of goods has become the most serious business of life. It is assumed by everyone and acknowledged as reasonable that every man should above all seek to "better himself" in any way he can so long as he plays fair with his neighbors. Such is the accepted way of our society and nobody is expected to complain about it. Nobody does so openly, but that is not the end of the matter. In addition to the public world in which we pursue our goods, every man lives in the inner world of his cares and anxieties which are attached to himself in a special way. He is a "living soul." He is the seat of an ambiguous dread which concerns his very existence. His days are numbered and their number measures a time in which he shall be cut off from "the land of the living," having found neither rest nor good. This prospect cannot but over-shadow his life and induce a permanent anxiety about it. When this anxiety which lies at the roots of human life is not acknowledged and shared, it alienates man from man and turns every man a stranger to his neighbor. The compassion of men one for another as "flesh and blood" is bread for their souls and as refreshing water to their spirits. When such com-passion is denied, each man suffers a devastating loneliness and the lonely man is an enemy of his fellowmen. He is con-vinced that his neighbors, preoccupied with goods and their benefits, no longer care for his life, or whether he be dead or alive. Being thus deprived of men's love, he turns against them with a lust for power. But more of this later.

2. *ORGANIZED POWER AND THE COMMON MAN*

The primary sources of power in our society are the power-machines. These machines are human constructions, products of human knowledge and ingenuity. They belong to vast systems which are produced through organizations of capital, management, labor, transportation, and sale. They merge into colossal interlocking organizations possessed of supernatural power. Such organizations control the use of scores of hundreds of millions of dollars. They employ thou-sands, scores of thousands, hundreds of thousands of people. They control the operations of power-machines doing the work of hundreds of thousands and millions of horses. All this is power passing imagination, virtually infinite power, *power produced by men and available to men.*

The fact that our environment contains supernatural powers, produced by men and under human control, makes for a new and wide-spread sense of virtual power. There is no limit set to aggrandizement. There is no conclusive reason why a man should not become a great man. There is no telling how far anyone will get. Hence there is a new flicker of ambition burning in the human soul, ready to turn into a consuming fire. Let a man "get a raise," or "put through a deal," or make a good speech, or win out in a local election, and he imagines himself climbing up and up to dizzy heights of glory. The slightest success is an occasion for megalomania. The teacher becomes an authority, the preacher moves to a cathedral, and the scientist revolutionizes human knowledge. Everyone but the village fool is on his way to a throne.

If, as commonly, it becomes unlikely, through no fault of one's own, that one should become a great man, the next best thing is to belong to a great organization. There is hardly a man who is not organized several times over. One belongs to the Chamber of Commerce, to the Republican Party, to the Rotary Club, to the Presbyterian Church, and to the American Legion. Another belongs to the Congress of Industrial Organizations, to the Democratic Party, to the Methodist Church, and the American Legion. Another belongs to the Writers' Guild, to the Socialist Party, to the committee of the Friends of Japan, to the Consumers' Union, and to the Unitarian Church, There are organizations for everybody's taste; anti-Semitic, anti-Catholic, anti-Negro, anti-capitalist, anti-government, anti-Russian, anti-British; there are associations of workers, farmers, teachers, dentists, tobacco-growers, milkmen, bakers, clothiers, scientists, and preachers. There are societies, leagues, and lobbies for someone's benefit and another's loss. And of course, there is "my country." And a man must not forget his race, his nationality, and his class. Hence, any man is a great man. He may be, and usually is, a nobody within the society to which he belongs, but still he has a sense of virtual omnipotence.

"The common man" enjoys a tremendous sense of power. He is a part of the society which contains colossal wealth and power. He is an American; America is a great and powerful country. Therefore, he is a great and powerful man. The colossal buildings around him, the factories vibrating with machine power, the billions of dollars he reads about, the vast systems of transportation, and the fabulous riches they carry hither and thither—all these tokens of power and predominance belong to *his* environment. They belong to his country and his people. He belongs to the country and the people which produced them. He and they belong together. They belong to him, and not to a Frenchman or an Indian. They are his. The power which produced them is his, and so is the power of the nation which possesses them. A man in our industrial society enjoys a vicarious but effective omnipotence which qualifies his whole existence.

The sense of power in a man who belongs to a powerful group is not always obtrusive. Any man one is likely to meet is moderate in both the sense of power and the desire to increase it. In fact, he is a mild man, amiable, and willing to live somewhere in the middle of the hierarchies of power. He is conspicuous in his willingness to "live and let live."

Still, he is not altogether free from envy toward one who is more prosperous and powerful than himself. He respects his superiors and treats his inferiors with a complacent contempt. He feels fairly content with his situation, but nothing he has or enjoys satisfies him. Envies and irritations crop up as it were from nowhere. There is a constant undertone of frustration, a constant desire to lord it over someone, a constant resentment because another is in the limelight, a constant pleasure at another's misfortune. There is a constant watchfulness, reserve, caution, and incipient hostility. Such traits in the decent citizen are inexplicable except as symptoms of thwarted ambition rooted in a sense of virtual omnipotence.

Such a vein of envy goes with a sense of unlimited rights. The common man in a powerful society has a right to his possessions and to much more than he now enjoys. There is no such thing as not having a right to what he has. And there is no limit to what he may rightfully have. He has a right to become the most powerful man in the community. The reason why he has not arrived at the top is that someone or some ones have stood in his way. Whence is this sense of right but from the sense of power? Right goes with power. The more powerful a man is, the more he is impressed with his rights. The sense of one's rights may not originate in the sense of power, but it does flourish with it. The sense of virtual omnipotence, appropriated from society, gives one the sense of a right to everything he can get. Everyone has a right to omnipotence, and that is because everyone might become omnipotent.

The common man's sense of virtual power finds expression also in his permanent impulse to blame others for his failure to realize his assumed potentialities. Every man has enough native intelligence to rise to the top of his business or profession. Every man has enough ability to make as much money as anyone else. He might have been the manager or president as well as this other man. He is "as good as the next man," and has all the virtues requisite for "top flight" success. There is nothing wrong with him. Hence his failure always involves another's guilt. If he does not have the opportunity to make the most of his unlimited powers, it is because others cling to their present advantage and block free competition which would surely end in his replacing them in a position of power and prestige. If he must continue to be a hireling and an underling, it is because others are intentionally oblivious to his merits. If he must live in dependence upon the will of others and allow his work to receive less than its due reward, it is because they are unjust men and also exploiters. In short, society withholds from him what is by right his own, and his neighbors are permanently guilty of not giving him his due. The sense of not receiving one's due and the corresponding conviction of guilt in others, are refractions of available power in the soul of the common man. Thus it is that every man is certain of his own essential innocence and ready to believe that anyone else is guilty. In our society where the sense of possible omnipotence is energized constantly by the powers around us, the temptation to impute guilt to everyone except ourselves is at once universal and irresistible. Our theoretical amorality has little effect upon this commonplace matter of fact.

The man who enjoys virtual omnipotence is habitually complacent, amiable, and even generous. But he is also condescending. Decent folk belonging to a superior race are full of kindness and solicitude towards those belonging to one that is inferior. They appreciate the quaint ways and droll virtues of the latter, and are full of benevolence towards them. They are chronic humanitarians, gods giving gifts and glowing bright with their own manifest goodness. The more good they do, the more they are established in their power and superiority and the less they will tolerate any pretension of equality from their inferiors. Thus we have whole nations, races, classes, with every Tom, Dick, and Harry in them, basking in a brilliant sun of power and superiority. In societies organized around the machines, the erstwhile arrogance of a minority is turned into a kindly conceit of masses who take it for granted that they are, simply speaking, superior. This ubiquitous superiority is generated and kept active by the colossal power in machine made societies.

The transmutations of the sense of power described above are not the products of "this ugly civilization." Human traits which lead men to enjoy vicariously power they do not possess, are to be found in the East as well as in the West, in the South as well as in the North. They can be explained in terms of psychological and sociological principles which are of universal validity. Mechanisms of "compensation," pride and prudence, "we-group" consciousness and group egoism, etc., which are ubiquitous in time and place, explain much of the behavior of the common man in our society as well as his behavior in any other culture. Still the unlimited powers and goods available in our society, as over against the limited powers and goods available in non-industrialized societies, have introduced a new dimension into the problem of power in our society. Our machines have made us virtually omnipotent. With them we can do all things. Hence we rely upon power with a new confidence and love it with a new zeal. Such confidence and zeal amount to a spiritual revolution.

The new sense of power, however, is utterly confused by a new and radical dependence upon ·complex systems of men and institutions. The more extensive and the more powerful these systems are, the more precarious is a man's existence among them. He is perennially apprehensive of probabilities of adverse exercises of power which shall upset his way of life and cause him devastating misery. In an ever threatened struggle between powerful divergent interests, he may wake up one day to find himself being crushed between forces over which he has little or no control. There may be reversals leading to depressions, unemployments, uprisings, dislocations of power, and even wars. In the midst of vast organizations of power, in the hands of fallible and corruptible men, the danger of radical loss is constant and debilitating.

The power in our environment, much of it integrated and in the hands of relatively few men, is passing imagination and potentially infinite; for what is beyond imagination shades into infinity. Who is a match for this new infinity? Before it, a finite man with his finite powers is as nothing, as mere dust in the balance. The instinct for self-preservation as well as the demands of ambition dictate that a man conform to the powers that be and seek promotion through their favor, rather than cross them and court ruin.

The better a man is adapted to the structure of power around him, the less he is aware of his impotence, If he has a good job and does it well, if he can afford and buys the goods offered at the stores, if he is subservient to the institutions which prosper through his work and patronage, if he thinks and acts as expected by men of power; in short, if he yields his soul to the structures of power which sustain him, he is a good man and lives a good life. The powers around him are the sources of a happy life as he knows it. They are the authors and custodians of the "American way" which means comfort, security and superiority. They give him what he wants. What if they also tell him what to want? In return for a painless consent, he lives freely and well. Thus voluntary self-identification with the systems of power by which he exists both conceals his impotence and establishes it. Weakness becomes bondage, and bondage is disguised as freedom. Nevertheless, bondage it is, and makes lust for power inevitable.

3. *THE NEW SUPERIORITY*

In machine dominated societies, those without whom the machines would not be able to run, are the superior people. Primary superiority belongs to those who organize the life of the machines: bankers, managers, executives, technical experts, supersalesmen, etc. In a secondary way, those who educate the sons and daughters of the superiors are superior educators. Preachers who preach to superior people are great preachers. The artists who sing or play before the superior people are *virtuosi* and breathtakers. Barbers who cut the hair of superior people are master barbers. There is no doubt of the superiority of those who serve the superiors. Authentic and unquestionable superiority today is a function of power over machines. Such superiority is, like the new power, ultimately quantitative, a superiority of "horse power." It is absolute because greater horse power is absolutely superior to lesser horse power. It is the bare superiority of mechanical power, which is something new.

Traditional pride is an evidence of despair rather than of power or superiority. Dependent upon powers beyond their control, subject to the rigors and terrors of nature, men often lifted up their heads against the gods and hurled defiance at them. Sometimes, they become "spiritual," that is, they cultivated an indifferent aloofness, showing their despair in contempt for goods and life alike. In any case, their pride was a bravado, obtrusive and invariably bitter. The proud man strutted about making enemies and inviting trouble. Sooner or later, either the gods or men "got him" and he went down.

The pride of the superior man today is made of other stuff. It is a complacent rather than rebellious pride, sure of its grip over nature and indifferent toward its gods. It is a pride unmixed with dependence, piety or fear. It is a pride born of a godlike power: symbolized by bountiful goods, nourished by comforts and enjoyments, and confirmed by the solid superiority of power itself. It is a pride too sure of itself even to make a show of itself.

Man's precarious existence in nature qualified his pride toward his fellowmen. A common exposure to misfortune culminating in death bound all men together in a common "humanity." It revealed a kinship and induced a compassion which confused the pride of the proud and reduced the meanness of the humble. A man had nothing he had not received and nothing he might not lose tomorrow. If he escaped loss in life, he could not escape the loss of life itself—which is the extreme poverty. Pride therefore was a foolish and wicked thing, a blindness to the essential equality of all men and a disloyalty toward "flesh and blood."

Today the gods have vanished and nature is reduced to a storage house for "raw material." Goods and power are neither given by the gods nor withdrawn by them. There is no Fortune which shall cause unpredictable loss and no Fate which shall overcome the man of power. There is no one to fear but men, and one need not fear them if one have sufficient power.

Pride in such a setting is a simple concomitant of power. Even the pride of mind and character is authenticated by machine made power. Pride now is a simple consciousness of power over men and money, free from the bravados of pretension and doubt. It is a gentlemanly pride, courteous and purring, and even benevolent. But, it is unmitigated by humility.

Men with machines are full of "humane sentiment." Their benevolence is wholesale and palpable, and they can point to it at all times with well justified pride. Almost every country possessed of the new power has experienced a sudden upsurge of benevolence. England, Germany, the United States have experienced powerful impulsions of humanitarian zeal. Everywhere, powerful men turn great philanthropists and privileged groups are converted to charity. Powerful men become benevolent men; but they will not jeopardize their hold on power. On the contrary, the benefits they confer upon others give them a divine title to their power and make it well-nigh immovable. In truth, their charities increase their power to virtual omnipotence. The gods owed not a little of their power to their generosity. They ruled by their goodness and power. When the new power came, the power of the gods was replaced by the superior power of men, and the goodness of the gods was transferred to men. It used to be hopeless to see the gods as at once good and powerful. They did not always come forth with the goods. But the men of power today do produce the goods and distribute them. Therefore, they are at once good and powerful. And their power is manifest in their goodness.

The transmutation of power into benevolence is never complete. Power remains and expresses itself also as condescension. Every new act of benevolence provides its doer with a new occasion for the exercise of his superiority. And since his superiority is due to his own virtues, there is no reason why he should not attribute the inferiority of the object of his benevolence to the lack of the same virtues in the other; and such a lack is automatically contemptible. The more good he does, the more he is confirmed in his contempt and justified in his superior power. Hence also, he is justified in trouncing any one who dares to challenge his power. Like a god crossed, his rage is thunder and lightning. He cannot countenance the presumption of his inferior beneficiaries who grasp at his power. He will let loose his power upon them and humble them; and if they will not be humbled, he will hurt them. Thus, his goodness vanishes into the thin air, rather it is retransformed into bare power which now deals violence and terror.

4. *THE NEW INHUMANITY*

Philanthropy among the prosperous does not exclude a profound indifference towards one's fellowmen. Men of power will pity the unfortunate, but they will not allow humanity to interfere with "business." When concerned with pecuniary interests, they recognize their neighbors not as human beings but as partners or competitors. They name men after their occupations and care little for them except in relation to profit and sundry benefits. They cultivate people, or neglect them, according to their ability to help, or hinder, them in "getting ahead." They forget a useless friend and try to be reconciled to an enemy who might become useful to them. Nobody is expected to blame them when they sacrifice the interests of their fellowmen in their quest for money and power. They assume that integrity is good in so far as it makes for prosperity and that right is subordinate to one's advantage. Thus it is that "good" men are habitually unjust; and being unjust, they are inhuman. Indeed, they are not barbarians. They do not assault their neighbor and batter him down. But they do overlook his humanity and use him as they use their machines, for the sake of power and goods. The inhumanity in such dehumanization is not always obvious. It is genteel and subtle as against cruelty among barbarians. Nonetheless, in its violation of the soul rather than the body, it is profoundly devastating. And one should not be surprised when it issues in cruelties far beyond the capacities of the traditional barbarian.

Even "social intercourse" among us is dehumanized. One's friends are those with whom one has fun. But how does one have fun? *Via* the machines. One goes riding, or to the movies; one listens to the radio; one goes dancing, dining, or drinking; one plays cards. People and machines alike are sought after in so far as they are joined together to fill our days with "fun." Men are not so much people as "company." The less we know of their fears and hopes, the better we like it. They are not permitted to tell us what is really on their minds and they are not supposed to "get serious" about anything. It is in bad taste to speak about anything that may be "bothering" them, anything personal or universal, especially if it is both.

People live, day after day, year after year, convinced that no one really cares for them. They know that they cannot share either joy or sorrow with their friends. They are not supposed to have private joys and they are not supposed to communicate private sorrows. Joy evokes resentment and sorrow produces a chill. "That's fine, old fellow—that's too bad, old fellow. But why do you have to come to me with it? Don't I have enough trouble of my own? Do *I* come running to you about it? What can I do? Besides, you know this is in bad taste. You should keep these things to yourself. No, this kind of thing is not done. If you want to have friends and to get along, keep your troubles to yourself. You never get people to like you better by telling them things that matter to you most."

The object of such a discourse, perhaps unspoken but not unheard, is an isolated and lonely man. He is not deceived by the smiles of salesmen, by the attention of interested neighbors, or even by the solicitude of professional lovers. In the midst of kindnesses and courtesies, he is ignored, neglected, and left alone. Hence it is that he and multitudes like him are alone among the crowds, homeless in their houses, without neighbors in their neighborhood and without friends among their friends; hungry while they eat, thirsty while they have a drink, ill while they are well, and joyless while having fun. Hence it is that they are insulted and injured, wounded in mind and sensibility, vaguely but powerfully anxious, unable to love or to be loved, prone to resentment and even cruelty. Such men suffer from a new and dehumanized inhumanity which is a deadly poison in our common life.

Neither beastliness nor the barbarian's physical cruelty is conspicuous in our society. Competence and proper conniving, and not headlong encounters, are the usual means to power and profit. Still, in their pursuit of goods and power, men lose even the barbarian's sense of humanity. "Flesh and blood" means nothing to them. "The bundle of life" means nothing to them. "The shadow of death" upon the faces of their fellowmen means nothing to them. They do not care if another man is joyful or in despair, dead or alive. They smile at him, but they do not love him. They talk with him, but they do not say anything. They work with him, eat with him, play with him, but they will not be bothered with *him*. He is an *it*, a part of organizations in which men are integrated with "machinery" and cease to act as persons. And in the nature of the case, he is used and exploited together with the rest of the materials which make for power and prosperity.

There is now a radical contradiction between a man as he is aware of himself and himself as others are aware of him. There is a public denial of him as the permanent man, a person subject to time and frustration, a soul subject to guilt and death, as the human being who would be acknowledged and loved. He realizes that his neighbor does not care to either love him or hate him, that he simply shuts the door to his face. And he is left alone in a wasteland, where life itself is a species of death. He is made desolate and barren within himself, turning into himself and upon himself, incapable of loving himself or anyone else. The new barbarians do not maim a man's body, they cripple his soul. They do not kill him, they only make him wish he were dead. They do not cut a limb, they make the whole man to wither. They simply deny a man's humanity, and tell him to go to the devil. And to the devil he goes.

5. *LUST FOR POWER*

The pursuit of power is one thing among friends, quite another among strangers. Among friends, power is instrumental to some proposed good. Even competition for superiority is for the sake of honor and esteem among friends. The impulse for power may be very strong, especially in communities where, according to the advertisers, there is no limit to the goods one may enjoy. But still, it is instrumental to some "apparent good."

Lust for power, power for its own sake, or the desire for mastery over men for the sake of mastery itself, is a product of estrangement. It appears among lonely men as a substitute for friendship. A man isolated from his fellowmen seeks mastery over them as the best means of security and contentment. He hopes to do with power what he has failed to do without love. The understanding of his fellowmen being no longer available, he seeks peace and security through power. He hopes that by power he will enter into a new and effective relationship with those around him, that by it he will overcome his isolation and enter into a community. He hopes that with mastery he will also receive the honor, esteem, and even the friendship of his fellowmen. There are numerous indications that he is on the right track. People flock around him, bow to him with much pleasing attention. Men treat the man of power with a deference they will not show to a friend. Thus it seems that power more than makes up for society lost through indifference. All seems to be better than well, and power is acknowledged commonly as a superior substitute for love and humanity.

But power does not remove one's isolation; it rather establishes it. In the midst of indifference, the more power one has, the more one is confronted with a radical insecurity. Indifference is changed into hostility, and one is not secure until the last enemy is destroyed. But since such an issue of power is remote and commonly impossible, one's insecurity becomes firm and permanent. The peace sought through power becomes a mirage which haunts a man only to sadden and madden him.

The isolated man is predestined to failure. His power is good for nothing. Nothing it realizes is good. There is nothing but itself which might be good. Therefore, *it* is the good. The isolated man is driven to find his good in power, rather, to seek power instead of the good. Both reason and its objects are pushed aside, and a "will to power," *sans* reason, *sans* good, *sans* hope, *sans* joy, becomes the dominating passion of the human spirit; not power over things which is a means, but a power over men which is now an end in itself. Now one lords it over others neither for security nor for any other advantage, but because it is absolutely gratifying to lord it over them. One will now jeopardize all good, and even life itself, for the sake of having others within the reach of one's arbitrary power. Neither the chafing and resentment of one's fellowmen, nor any palpable danger of rebellion and violence, nor one's own isolation and misery, nor all the bitterness that goes with tyranny, nor any other evil or prospect of evil, including death, will induce one to forego one's mastery and to seek the peace of a shared humanity. The will to power has now replaced the love of life itself. One would rather be a dead lord than a live man. A stupid bargain this is, but it is the only one available to an outcast.

It is axiomatic, although not too well phrased, that all men want to be happy. Happiness is a subjective state which accompanies both the successful pursuit and the enjoyment of some apparent good. Moreover, happiness is possible only in a community. Hence, human powers lead to happiness only when they are employed toward some apparent good in the setting of mutual care and concern among men. When such a setting is absent, men use their energies not toward happiness but toward domination. Power is used not with the prospect of some good it will accomplish but toward a mastery which is an end in itself.

There is a love of power, and there is a lust for power; and these two are not the same. The enjoyment of power in pursuit of some good is one thing, the joyless will to power for its own sake is quite another. It is one thing to strive for self-preservation, quite another to strive for domination. It is one thing to use power as moved by hungers and fears, quite another to use it as moved by hunger for power and fear of the lust for power in others. It is one thing to seek power for self-respect among one's neighbors; it is quite another to seek it for domination over strangers and enemies. There is a love of power which is bound up with the love of life among our fellowmen. There is a lust for power which cares neither for life nor for fellowman. The second is a perversion and corruption of the first. It is a contradiction both of nature and of reason. The lust for power is not an exercise of humanity. It is a suspension of it. It is the consequence of indifference among persons, or a radical repudiation of humanity. So long as the love of power and the lust for power are confused one with the other, so long as men believe that the latter is a straight manifestation of human nature, it will be impossible to understand the problems of power among men or to propose effective solutions to them.

The new environment produced by machines has inflamed men's desire for power and produced a new social situation in which the transmutation of love to lust works with a new and dramatic energy. It is impossible to understand the concrete expressions and the special virulence of lust in our time without observing men's behavior in their new setting among machines and social organizations dependent upon machines. Hence any adequate study of lust in our time is possible only in terms of "modern society" and its effects upon the human mind. No abstract view of "human nature" can give us a proper knowledge of lust and its workings among us.

Nevertheless, lust is not *caused* by anything in a man's environment. Men do not lust by necessity. Their lusting is a *human* response to their setting, and as such it presupposes a liability to lust. The main purpose of this book is to examine this liability, and thus to explain the transmutation of love to lust.

CHAPTER III

Lust in the Making

1. *A STRANGE DISPROPORTION*

PEOPLE HAVE A peculiar impulse to "make a mountain out of a mole hill." They exaggerate both the good and the evil that happen to them. They respond to a good as though it were the Good and to an evil as though it were the Evil, thus making themselves ludicrous both to themselves and to others. But in doing this, they also reveal a characteristic of man without which we understand neither his life nor his ways. The following fable is intended to suggest this truth and to prepare the reader for the analysis of lust in the rest of this chapter.

A young economist has just read a paper to a gathering of his colleagues. They have responded to him with interest and obvious pleasure. Several of them have risen to their feet and spoken at some length to the effect that it was a learned, original and very illuminating paper. One of the older gentlemen has gone so far as to prophesy that the writer of this paper is a promising young scholar from whom great things are to be expected. There has been a good discussion of the subject at hand, with questions and remarks, and the meeting has ended on a happy note of approval with smiles and handshakes.

Now, all this was very good for our author. He has done a creditable piece of work. His prestige has been enhanced and he has found favor with his fellowmen. It is very likely that he shall now belong to the society of scholars with established reputations, and that these shall receive him as an equal, listening to his views with a new attention and respect. It certainly looks as though he had launched upon a career of increasing success and usefulness. Besides, he might have his article published in the *National Journal of Economics.* From then on, there is no telling what might happen. The thing might catch the eye of the Dean of the School of Economics in one of the Great universities. There might be an offer of a Chair with considerably higher salary. The Administration of his own college might hear about it and decide to keep him at any cost. Even the Government might enter into the fray and offer to make him Chief Consultant in Trade Relations with South America. He might be offered as high as fifteen thousand dollars a year. But in the long run it might be better to accept a Chair with an eight thousand dollar salary. That might be more secure, and besides life might be simpler than if he lived in Washington. One must not underestimate the advantages of an academic career. As for a choice between a Big university and a college, it might be wise to stay in a college. There will be less demand made on his time and energy, and he will be able to study and write more than if he were in a university. He shall be asked to give Special Lectures at the universities. These Lectures shall be published and there shall be no doubt that he is an Authority.

Now, all these possibilities are real, and our author has some reason for his elation. His reflections may be somewhat exaggerated but they are not altogether absurd. He does have good prospects and we ought not to deny him his enjoyment of them. However, there is more to his happiness. As he contemplates his success and his hopes for the future, a strange and absolute thrill takes possession of him. The contents of his article, from the title, "The Economic Prospects of Brazil," to the last sentence, "There is not a country in the world with a future as bright and glorious as that of our sister Republic beyond the Equator," come to him over and over again, now in one order and then in another, like pure and perfectly polished jewels. There is no doubt that he has written the perfect paper. When he re-sees in his mind the lighted faces of his colleagues as they listened to him read, and as he re-hears in his soul their comments made afterwards, all his doubts and disaffections vanish away into the void and he is left with a complacence which is both absolute and boundless. He is as a man lying down in the fields on a bright summer day. All is warmth and light and peace and a quiet but infinite joy. The shadows of his past life are gone forever, and the future, no matter how he sees it, shall be a brilliant and eternal Day. He has not only seen good, he has met the Good beyond Evil.

Eighteen months have elapsed, and our economist has read another paper before the same gathering. (By the way, nothing much has come of his previous success. He has had his article on Brazil published, but he has received only one letter about it, and that from a Brazilian Attaché in Washington, who thanked him in behalf of his Government and expressed hope for closer economic relations between his Country and the Great country of the United States of America. As for a Big university and the Administration of his own college, they have said nothing. In the meantime he has been made Associate Professor; for the usual reasons. Otherwise, during these eighteen months, life has gone on as usual. All is well, but not very much better.) This time the response of his colleagues is on the cool side. Almost as soon as he begins, their eyes settle down to a lifeless gaze and their faces grow dark. Every time he looks at his audience, he sees somebody jerking an arm as though trying to glance at his wrist watch. A few are preoccupied with keeping their eyelids up. There is some coughing and moving about in the seats. It is a dull and tiresome hour, and the more he works, the less anybody seems to care. When he has finished reading, there are no questions. This paper is on "Economic Cooperation in South America." But the first gentleman to speak makes some remarks on the Philippine Islands. The second one shifts the scene to Spain. The third brings in Russia; and when the Big Bear enters the room, both the paper and South America are forgotten. More people express themselves, but the discussion becomes confused. Soon the second allotted hour is consumed, and after a few handshakes and inane remarks addressed at the Reader, the scholars go home: all except the Reader. He walks out, turns to the right, and goes Nowhere.

It has been a painful afternoon. The Reader has failed. The many hours he had spent gathering his data and composing his paper, complete with facts, figures, and footnotes, had been wasted. Those jaded chairwarmers have not been impressed. They have, in fact, acted as though he were a pedant and a bore. It was all his fault. He had altogether too many computations in his paper. His sentences were too long and complicated; the organization of his material also was at fault. He turns sentence after sentence over in his mind; then he thinks over his paragraphs and sections; then he throws everything around, several times and in several orders, until he arrives at disorder itself. Doubtless, the paper was not very good; they must have sensed it from the very beginning. There is no question that his reputation has suffered. Maybe there will be some talk, and the Administration, or even the Students, will hear about it. No immediate harm is likely to come from the Administration, but there is no telling when and how this business can hurt him and change his entire Future for the worse. The Students might begin to question his competence and resist his authority in their own infernal way. For years to come, he might have fewer students in his elective courses and it might become a fixed opinion on the campus that he is not much of a teacher. He might lose his nerve and become a piece of academic deadwood.

Such reflections, disheartening as they are, do not quite explain the actual gloom which has entered our reader's soul. There is no congruity between his fears and the inner Desolation which has overtaken him. He has not failed once; he has become a failure. His past successes have become as nothing, and his future is one prolonged darkness. As he walks on aimlessly, seeing barely enough to keep clear of the obstacles on his way, he is a lost little man, without love and without friends, without memories and without expectations, an empty self closed to the world, with a monotonous and enervating ache as the only sign that he is still alive. There is neither quantity nor quality to this Gloom. His hurt and pain cannot be compared with any caused by the many mishaps in this life. They have only an indirect and irrational connection with the evil that has just happened to him. By any count, his misfortune was a finite loss and his unhappiness with it should be limited. But that is not the case. This dull, dispassionate, all-consuming Melancholy in him is as absolute as it is unique; an impression of Evil beyond good.

Our economist is now a Full Professor. But even that has not effected a revolution in his life. He is like most of his colleagues, a good scholar and teacher, and in general, a good man. His responses to the two situations described above were, of course, strange, but they were far from being due to some peculiar mental quirk of his own. They are the kind of response with which all men of a sound mind meet, more or less often, the goods and evils that pass through their lives. Of course, the more serious and consequential the occurrence, the more likely it is to evoke an absolute response. A sudden change of fortune for riches or poverty, victory or defeat, good or bad reputation, good or bad health, etc., is most likely to arouse metaphysical passions in us. But even trivial events are often accompanied by a strange Gloom or Light which is absolute. A man finds a pen with boundless satisfaction and loses a pair of rubbers with infinite disgust. A friendly grin makes for Sunshine; an uninterested look makes for a Dreary Day. There are times when, to have one's way in the slightest matter, is to achieve absolute power, and to be frustrated in the slightest intention is to become impotent. A new hat or a good meal produces utter contentment, whereas the old hat or a poor meal reduces us to sheer misery. And so it goes through the vicissitudes of our existence. Goods come laden with the Good and evils with the Evil. Everything signifies the absolute. It speaks to us of things final and ultimate, even while it remains in the world of more or less. Everything is both finite and passing; better or worse than something else. But also, everything happens to us with a strange influence, as though it were a matter of life and death.

It is not enough to observe that men have a confirmed and apparently irresistible tendency to see the relative as absolute. One must try to understand this incurable addiction of man to the absolute. If we assume that all objects are relative, we must explain the inner alchemy which transforms them into bearers of an absolute. The opinion that such alchemy is the work of the imagination is not as illuminating as it sounds. Images can be increased, and they can be decreased, but they cannot be transformed into sources of an absolute Fear, or Hope. If we say that the absolute is due to the emotions, to panic aroused by the vicissitudes of our existence, we are no nearer understanding the inner life. We are still in the dark as to the nature of the impulse which turns a fear into a panic. It is no more helpful to propose that the disproportion of the inner to the outer world is due to the deficiency of our reason. Reason can misjudge relations, as alas it does only too often. But it cannot transmute the relative into an absolute. Men are more or less intelligent, and they judge relations more or less rightly. But the juxtaposition of the relative and the absolute has nothing to do with calculation. Relatives do not add up to an absolute, and an absolute cannot be divided into a set of relatives. Arithmetic has nothing to do with this matter. No fear explains Fear, and no hope can turn into Hope. Fear and Hope are responses to something other than the objects around us. Hence their origin must be sought elsewhere.

2. *OF LIFETIME: PERSONS AND THINGS*

There is no explaining the juxtaposition of the absolute and the relative in human life in terms of goods and evils. A man preoccupied with this good and that evil, either present or to come, cannot be the source of the absolute. As a man to whom things happen, together or one after another, he is in no relation to anything absolute. He is a scene of events which belong to the world of objective relations. Goods come, remain for a while, and go their way. Even the pain and pleasure they cause belong to an indefinite procession of events. Their intensities vary; but still they belong to the world of variables and there is no reason, in terms of their occasions, for why they should not be more or less intense. All "psychological" events, in so far as they are responses to goods and evils in life, are objective occurrences sharing the principle of relativity valid for everything in our world.

To a man preoccupied with his environment of goods and evils, all events, eating, working, playing, and sleeping, fall into different times, each with its own beginning and ending. There is a time of day and a time of night. There is a time to buy and a time to sell, a time to work and a time to play. There are good times and hard times, times of success and times of failure. All events, whether objective or subjective, from the greatest to the least, have their times. Man alone, in relation to things, has no time which is his time.

In relation to objects, man is without his own time and unaware of his own being. Everything around him moves; his own body moves; but he is motionless, and unperceived. He is the locus of innumerable experiences, but he has no substance, no being apart from the objects around him. He himself is a bottomless void being occupied by an endless succession of experiences with their own several times.

When such a being responds to the relative as though it were something absolute (which is a contradiction), we have no recourse but to theorize that the true absolute is *the time of his own life*. Each man has his beginning and his end; and to each man his beginning and his end mark out an absolute time which is the time of his being. The time of each man is related not only to the times of the beings around, but also to a time which is prior and posterior to himself. Each moment in his life is related not only to the moments of the durations of other beings, but also to the moment of the beginning and the moment of the end of his own life; and this beginning and this end are upon a dotted line of time for which no beginning and no end are discernible.

The time of man is radically different from the time of things. A thing exists without regard to its beginning and to its end. A river flows without a memory of its beginning in the past and its end in the future. It flows on a year or a thousand years, without concern about the span of its existence. A tree may have ten, or a hundred, or a thousand years to live. But it stands oblivious to its lifetime, marking only the times of its life. An animal, so to speak, "struggles for existence." It may resist its predatory neighbor and fight for its survival. But it does not live in its lifetime. The beginning and the end of its life are apart from the succession of events in its daily existence. At one time it eats; at another, it plays; at another, it sleeps; at still another, it mates. But these different instances of its life have no relation to its birth or its death. There is no living bond, not even an objective, clock-time bond, which binds them together in relation to its lifetime. An animal doubtless has memory. It also anticipates the immediate future. But the span of its awareness does not coincide with its lifetime. Unaware of its lifetime, the animal may resist death at any time, but death does not qualify moments of its life.

This mountain will last a million years as against this flower which will fade away tonight. But, the mountain sees no advantage in its longevity; and the flower is unmoved by the brevity of its day. The flower does not say: "I live but a day. But the mountain also will one day fall down and cease to be forever." It is only man who contrasts a day with many years, and finds them both a vanity. It is only man that contrasts a day and many years alike with endless time, and finds them both as the twinkling of an eye. Man alone has a lifetime, a time circumscribed by his beginning and his end; a time in which a being confronts nonbeing, and recognizes the absolute difference between being alive and not being alive.*

The time of a thing is irrelevant to the times of its existence. It exists as though it did not begin and as though it were not going to end. It exists through a period of time. But being indifferent to its beginning and its end, it is related to one moment as it is related to any other. It does not bind the times together into a time in which one moment differs from another by virtue of its unique relation to the beginning and the end of its existence. Thus a thing is essentially nontemporal. It does not exist in the present as over against its past and its future. It exists timelessly, and therefore it is a thing and not a person. It has a succession of states but no history.

The fact that man has had a beginning and will have an end conditions and qualifies his total existence.

I was born. I was not, and then I was. I am, but I was not. I am, but I shall not be. Having not been, I am; I am coming to be what I was not; I am coming not to be what I was; I am coming not to be; I virtually am not. I was not, and

* In the following pages, "being" and "nonbeing" are used in a non-Platonic sense. In the Platonic tradition, "Being" is the idea or form which all beings have in common. It is "being in general" which is eternal, as over against particular beings which come and go without adding to or taking away from Being. We, on the other hand, are concerned with individual beings, and especially with men. In Platonic usage, a man is, in that he participates in Being. In our usage, a man does not participate in Being. His being is unique in the sense that he is himself and nobody else. When he ceases to be, his being is turned into "non-being" in that he no longer exists. We apologize to the Platonists for using their words in our own way. However, we also have a right to "being"! We earnestly hope that with this word of caution the reader will have no difficulty with our language.

We have also used the word "existence." But we are not concerned with the contrast between essence and existence, or between thought and existence. Our discussion has to do with the existence of a man and with his nonexistence. Existence, in the traditional sense, is unthinkable; because everything as thought is an idea. Existence, in our sense, may be unthinkable; but it is also indispensable! We suspect that a man's existence is a necessary condition of his thinking. We beg the reader to forget "existentialism" when reading our book. We are not concerned with the "existential" in the sense of the subjective, the concrete, the irrational, the non-teleological, the suprahistorical, etc. We are not arguing with Hegel. Our debate is with those who

I shall not be. I am as he who was not and shall not be. Therefore, I act necessarily not as I-am-and-was-and-ever-shall-be, but as I-am-and-was-not-and-shall-not-be.

There is no activity without spending time. You will spend more time for an end which seems to promise the greater good. It is worth your while to spend the afternoon in going on a walk; it is not worth your while to spend it in the movies. You may use time doing this; but not doing that. It is no good to waste half your life doing this, but it is no waste at all to spend all the rest of your days doing that. If you had three lives to live instead of one, you might give much more time doing this or that; in fact, you might start doing something quite different. If you had five hundred years ahead of you, you might stop worrying about whatever is worrying you; you might go on a long vacation; you might start studying music; you might liquidate your business; or you might take to drinking. You might do anything, and you would do everything differently from the way you do it now. If you had only a year of life left, again you would perhaps

---

consider man's "lifetime" (to be explained later) irrelevant to the conduct of his life. Hence, we emphasize "existence" as over against the non-existence of an individual human being.

We sympathize with the "nausea" of the French existentialists. But we find little illumination in their impulsive nihilism and their plea for a bare freedom of unconsidered action. We have tried to *think out* the misery of man in the modern world.

We are also afraid that we shall be misunderstood with regard to our use of the word "death." We are not interested in death itself, which is simply uninteresting. We are interested in it as the limit of a man's "lifetime." Death confronts us with our finitude; and (so we shall argue), our finitude conditions our existence as human beings; so much so that to ignore death is to think without a clue which is indispensable for understanding our behavior.

We have used other words like person, freedom, guilt, the Shadow, the Void, Dread, ambiguity, science, which are likely to be misunderstood if they are construed in terms of common usage. But, we earnestly hope that one who thinks these words in the contexts of our arguments, and of the book as a whole, will have little difficulty with them. Our thought is simple in the extreme. We are sorry that language itself is not simple. We have had "something to say," and we have said it nearly as well as we were able to do it.

do something different and do it differently from the way you would do it now. If you were without beginning or end, Heaven only knows what you would or would not do. It is most likely that you would be like the angels who cannot be imagined seriously as doing anything at all. If you were without beginning or end, time would be very cheap, in fact, worthless. Then you would perhaps spend a thousand years fixing a chair, and another thousand writing a letter. If you were without beginning or end, how would you go about learning a profession, or making money, or courting and getting married? These activities take time. But how much time? How much time in a lifetime without beginning or end? How would you measure time in a boundless setting?

We measure our times within the setting of our lifetime. Our doings during our days and years are in times which are fragments of our lifetime. These are the fragments of the time of our existence, and the deeds we do during them are our deeds as those who exist for a while. Our finitude conditions the tempo of our deeds and the passion with which they are done. The impulse in the pursuit of any good whatsoever is informed with a sensibility derived from our finitude. We allow ourselves so much time for attaining this or that because we shall exist so long and no longer. The fact that we shall exist so long and no longer is essential to our life and to all our deeds. And it determines the essence of our inner life.

A person is one whose lifetime determines the times of his life. The primary marks of personal existence are inexplicable apart from such determination. A person is aware of himself as a continuing entity. But where does he get this sense of continuity? When he objectifies himself, that is, when he considers his various experiences, he knows only a succession of events. He counts and compares, but he finds no continuing self. His own duration as an indivisible entity disappears and he cannot make anything of himself as a perduring self. When he places the times of experiences in the settings of the times of objects, he ceases to have any continuity whatsoever. It is only when he contemplates the vicissitudes of life in the setting of his lifetime that he apprehends his own individual essence. It is only thus that he knows himself as himself and acknowledges the unique meaning of his existence in relation to the world of objects. Not even his body could give him this sense of his perdurance without his recognition that he has a lifetime.

A person is sometimes defined as one who remembers and anticipates, entertains purposes, and strives toward some good. It is true that a person does all this. But the question is, why does a person do it? Is it not because the good must be attained and enjoyed in the setting of one's lifetime? Every good is sought after in time, and this time is one's lifetime. Remembering, anticipating, planning, purposing, are all done in view of time. What time? Certainly not the time of objects. Equally certainly, in terms of the time of one's life. The past is remembered as past, the future is anticipated as future. One plans in the light of the past and one purpose for the future. But what past and what future? Past and future as circumscribed by one's birth and one's death. Indeed, we plan for our children, for institutions which shall outlast us, for the nation, and even for mankind. But in so far as *we* propose to execute our plans, we work within the setting of our lifetime. A man must provide for the future of his family; and he has a limited time in which to do it. Therefore, he must work now or tomorrow; the day after tomorrow may be too late. This statesman must work for the peace and prosperity of his people. He must do it now. Tomorrow he will be gone. A person cannot but plan with reference to his own lifetime.

Again, a person is defined as a responsible agent. A person is one who acknowledges an obligation and his duty to conform to it. And when he sets out to do his duty or affirms his guilt in not having done it, he exists and perdures as a being other than all objects. It is in responsible action that the real present divides the past from the future and reveals the existent person. But one cannot stop at this point. The present is not only a line dividing the past from the future. It is not a line that opposes any past to any future. It is an enduring line in the setting of the duration of one's lifetime. And this line is the locus of personal existence. Our duties appear in the context of our lifetime. To be guilty is an evil akin to death. In fact, the prospect of death and the burden of guilt are inseparable. When finitude is ignored, so is guilt ignored. But of course neither is thereby removed. A person is a responsible person, and the manner of his responsibility is a function of his finitude.

A person is a being who uses symbols, and with symbols achieves language, society, science, religion, art and philosophy. With symbols he achieves a peculiarly human freedom from "brute fact," and transcends his environment as a person. Thus he exercises a creativity which is of the essence of culture. But then, one has to take only one discerning look at human culture in order to realize that its deepest and most persistent sources are in man's finitude. The creative impulse cannot be understood except in the context of the human lifetime. Not one of the heroes of the race, including Karl Marx, can be understood except as a human being, that is, as one who knows the deadly sting of finitude which nevertheless makes the difference between a person and "brute creation."

A person is one who cares for his fellowmen as men. He is one whom his neighbor recognizes as a man who knows him as he knows himself. But how does a man know himself? A man knows himself as one whose lifetime is radically different from the times of objects. Hence, one man can know another only when he knows himself as one whose time is not commensurate with the times of objects.

The above is not intended to be a complete description of a person. And certainly our argument has not reached its end. But enough has been said, for the present, to suggest that the finitude of human life qualifies the totality of it. In man, being and nonbeing confront one another, and life as human is the consequence of this confrontation.

3. *OF BEING, HAVING AND BEHAVING*

Human behavior cannot be understood in terms of the pursuit of finite goods. In this world of "means and ends," which constitute the realm of having, there is an end which is the end of having because it is the end of being. All ends sought and had are within the bounds of the absolute beginning and absolute end of a man's existence. Being is the condition of having and the finitude of being qualifies all human having. If we simply were, without a lifetime bounded by time without life, we would have differently from our having now, and differently also from the manner in which we now do not have. We would neither seek nor possess as we do now. Angels do not grip their harps, neither do the saints cling to their crowns. Heavenly possessions are gifts and there is no danger of losing them. They are acquired without lust and possessed without grasping. Angels play their harps by nature and saints wear their crowns by grace. Being safe in their possession, they are not attached to either crown or harp. The angels simply play their harps in praise of God and the saints wear their crowns before Him. The former cannot imagine themselves without their harps, neither can the latter imagine themselves without their crowns. Neither angels nor saints can conceive of themselves as being without having or as having without being. They do not fear for their lives, and they do not fear for their possessions. They neither "assert" themselves nor repudiate themselves. They neither exploit their fellow beings, nor annihilate themselves with their possessions. Having no lifetime, they know no desire for anything and no despair of attaining it. There is no moment in which they lack anything, and no end which will prevent their getting anything. They do not scheme or calculate. No angel wants another's harp, and no saint wants another's crown. Each one has as though he did not have and does not have without wanting. Since angels and saints simply are, they also simply have. Their being is without dread, and their having is without lust. They are and have in a way that is radically different from our being and having. They *have* differently because they *are* differently. Their having is a function of their being, as is true also of us.

To be is essential! This is true of all being, and it is true of man. Where being is not, nothing is. Being is the condition of all good, even though being is not good *for* anything. Yet, being is good for everything, since without it there would be no good at all. All goods are good for something. They never are good for nothing or good for everything. Being alone is such a good, and no good. As the condition of all good, it is uniquely and absolutely good. But, since it does not belong in a system of goods, it is no good at all. A man cannot love life as he loves a steak or a car. What is often called the "love of life" consists in having an enormous appetite. Life is not and cannot be enjoyed like things because life is not a thing among things. On the other hand, without life there is no enjoying anything. Thus, life is absolutely valuable, but all other goods are relatively valuable. To be and to have are goods of two different orders.

It is exceptionable and pernicious to argue that since existence is not a good among goods it is not in any sense good. Utilitarians, pragmatists and other less theoretical worldlings completely dissociate the problem of being and the problems of having. They are interested in having and not in being. Idealists and other noble but not too clear-minded souls argue that the "good life" is better than life itself, so that a man should rather die than live wickedly. Moralists identify the good with doing one's duty and they also scorn the problem of being as irrelevant to the conduct of life. The most prevalent moral axiom of our time, upheld by all types of promoters of the good life, is that being and having are two different matters. But then—if one does not exist, one can neither have nor enjoy any good whatsoever. One may not wish to live miserably. But to live well cannot be made a substitute for living at all, as one might substitute one hat for another. To live well is better than to live poorly. But it is nonsense to say that the good life is better than life itself. A man values a good life but he also values life without which he cannot live in any way at all.

The living love life necessarily. The love of life is the awareness of the absolute opposition between being alive and being dead. In man, it is to *be* alive, so that being alive and loving life are the same thing under two aspects. A man loves life in the very fact that he is alive. The love of life goes with a man's peculiar realization in his being as against his nonbeing. A man's being is to him absolutely good. It is good as over against his nonbeing, which is evil. This good which is the good of being, a good peculiar to being as being, is a metaphysical good, acknowledged as the necessary condition of all empirical goods, a good owned not by experience but by being. A man by being knows being as good; in this knowledge, to be and to know are the same.

True enough, the good of being is known only in the enjoyment of goods; but the enjoyment of goods is also an enjoyment of being. Goods would not be good as they are good were it not that the good of being is embedded in their goodness as goods. Were it not for the love of being, which in our case is inseparable from the dread of nonbeing, goods would not be good as they are good to us. A harp to an angel is not as is a piano to a man. The worth of the piano is proportionate to the effort one has put into mastering it. Such effort has taken time. Time is lifetime which is the measure of one's being. Into one's enjoyment of playing the piano enters his total being under the shadow of nonbeing. The good of being and the good of playing the piano are separable one from the other. Hence the good of playing a harp is not for an angel the same as is the good of playing the piano to a man. All one has to do is to watch them perform. The angel is sitting erect and twanging away with mathematical precision and unchanging placidity. The man is bent over his instrument, staring at the keys, playing with a peculiar seriousness and intensity, as though the sounds he makes are intended to utter the unutterable. No man can behave as an angel, and no angel can live as a man. Being and behaving are of one piece.

All that a man would do must be done in limited time. He wants a decent house with all "the modern conveniences," a job which is lucrative without being too wearing, security in the possession and use of his property, and his enjoyment of wife, friends, and children. Now, it is of decisive importance that he does not have an indefinite amount of time in which to acquire these "blessings of life." He does not care to have a good job after he is sixty. He does not want to live in a tenement house until he is fifty. He must get married before it is too late. He must acquire all he wants in good time because after a while he will not be able to do justice to the good things of life, and heaven knows when he will be cut off from life and from everything. The sooner he comes to possess the means of happiness, the longer he will be happy. There is just so much time. The more goods one has for a longer time, the more happiness one will achieve. Men's actual zeal in the pursuit of goods is a function of their finitude.

A man does not have forever in which to accomplish his ends. Not only that, but also it is not certain that a man will have a tomorrow in which to acquire and to enjoy. It is likely that a man will continue to live ten more years. But there is no guarantee of that. What one is sure of is only the present. What a man does not have now, he may never have. What he has now, tomorrow he may lose forever. Thus, having and not having are in the setting of being and not being. Human seeking, having and enjoying, are what they are in relation to the togetherness of being and nonbeing in the life of man.

The limited nature of our time invests our existence with a peculiar quality. "Now or never" generates an impetuosity out of proportion to any good in view. Every good pretends to be an absolute. Neither the desire for possessions nor the enjoyment of them corresponds to how much good they are in relation to other goods. The amount of good in goods cannot be determined with any objective measure. The force of a man's grip upon his wallet does not correspond to the measure of its contents. The force of his grip is derived from the meeting of being and nonbeing in him. The manner of human having, in short, is a function of the peculiar manner of human being.

This girl "would rather die" than go to a party in last season's dress. That man would "be damned" rather than forego his drink or his radio. That woman would "kill herself" rather than send her child to "that school." Such sentiments are mostly exaggerations. However, they indicate a constant proneness to respond *in extremis*. They are telltale evidence that things sought or avoided have a constant tendency to become "matters of life and death." Having has the glory of being, and not having it as empty as nonbeing itself. The most trivial decision appears as though it were to be made once for all. For one moment, one is suspended between everything and nothing, between realization and frustration, between heaven and hell. Everything, rather life itself, is at stake. In having or not having, in having that or not having that, being confronts nonbeing. It is as though human having or not having were human being or not being in disguise, as though being were transmuted into having and having retained the absolute nature of human being.

Today, there are indefinite possibilities of power, possession, and enjoyment; and there is a definite limit to the time in which a man must acquire and enjoy. In our day, the goods a man might accumulate are virtually infinite, but the time in which he might accumulate them is finite. Finite men are potentially infinite in the world of machines. Being remains circumscribed according to nature, but having has burst the bonds and is racing toward infinity. Men who carry the mark of death are confronted with opportunity for infinite having. If they were immortal, they would go on and on, accumulating to their heart's content, without haste and without waste. Maybe they would not accumulate at all. But being mortal, they must accumulate all they can while they can. Hence, they accumulate the finite with a zeal generated by the infinite. The passion generated by the ideal infinite enters into their accumulation of the finite and turns their whole existence into nonsense.

Being and nonbeing opposed in man have always generated a lust which is man's undoing. However, today, when accumulation points to infinity, the temptation to find being in having has assumed a new force, and few are they who resist it, much less overcome it.

4. *THE INFINITE AND THE ETERNAL*

The absolute impulse toward multiplication and accumulation is inexplicable in terms of finite needs. There is nothing in nature or reason as concerned with finite goods which explains the lust in the human pursuit of goods. Man as a locus of needs and satisfactions is not a proper agent of lustful activity. It is unnatural and irrational that men seeking goods should seek an infinite number with an absolute passion.

Being is the only absolute, and "eternal life" is the only rational object of an absolute impulse. Hence, the quantitative infinite can be nothing else than the eternal reconstituted. The concern with a time-full eternal is replaced with lust for a timeless infinite. The dread of being in nonbeing is dissipated, at least apparently, through a preoccupation with things which can be multiplied indefinitely. Personal existence is repudiated in favor of a process whose only contents are an indefinite multiplicity of experiences. Thus the radical dread conjoined with our existence is set aside and men live impersonally, that is, impervious both to being and to not being. The life of man becomes a succession of successes which are failures and failures which are forebodings of disaster. However, the pursuit of goods is carried on with undiminished energy. The mind is diverted from the vacuum of endless time by the virtual plenum of experienced and promised things; and thus a new infinity replaces the old eternal as the object of man's attention and the end of his labors.

Man is a "living soul" who anticipates his death. His first love is "eternal life" which is the unattainable. But the unattainable has disappeared and is replaced by the attainable which is the new infinite. Rather, the Unattainable has been transformed into the Attainable. Unattainable Life, life in which being has overcome nonbeing, is now replaced by an attainable life, a life characterized by a virtual infinity of appropriation. Unattainable bliss, the bliss of eternal life, is now replaced by an attainable happiness of minimum need and maximum enjoyment. What now is the good life but a maximum pleasure with goods? What is bliss but a maximum of enjoyments? What is the good society but one in which the greatest number of sentient beings enjoy the greatest number of goods? The good is now a matter of nontemporal quantity, and this quantity is virtually infinite. Even qualities are quantitatively measured, and both quality and quantity are nontemporal, that is, irrelevant to man's lifetime or his personal existence. The unattainable is changed into the attainable by doing away with the person.

Preoccupied with the goods available in our industrial society, men are done with chasing after an ambiguous and never-attained eternal. The spiritual life, with all its praying, philosophizing and poetry, failed to move men one inch away from the shadow of death. Besides, it produced neither food nor drink. It only fixed the heart and mind of man upon a precarious destiny and made him serious throughout his days. Now the situation of man is changed. There is food where there was hunger, health where there was disease, and comfort instead of drudgery. Goods keep pouring out from our factories and make for a standard of living which was beyond the means of even the gods of our fathers. And there is no end in sight. Hence men are only too glad to forget about their lifetime and to live having the time of their life. Men know where their bread is buttered, and so do their leaders. Hence the thoughtful and the thoughtless alike have rolled over and shut their eyes to the eternal.

The displacement of the eternal by the infinite leads to a dissolution of the person. The once-for-allness of personal existence becomes unreal and incomprehensible. People exist as objects and their existence is identical with the existence of things. They are parts as things are parts and replaceable as things are replaceable. They are specimens of a particular kind of thing, and so long as there are things of their kind, no one may reasonably care whether they themselves exist or do not exist. As no one cries over a discarded car if one has another that is just as good or perhaps better, no one may reasonably cry over the loss of one man so long as there are so many others to do his work. Persons may come, and persons may go. But there remain science, technology, civilization; goods, ideas, ideals; patterns, processes, problems; possibilities, probabilities, progress; cultural heritage, the exploitable environment, the enduring mankind. The objective world will be there indefinitely, with its infinite contents as experienced continuously by forthcoming generations of men and women. Neither the life nor the good of any particular man is crucial or even a serious matter.

The replaceability of men and women is an enormously consequential principle of our society. The person who produced our culture, the indivisible and dynamic essence whose destiny agitated the souls of men, is now barely discernible. The human being who agonized about the eternal and lived under its shadow, must now hide himself from both himself and his fellowmen. He dare not look at himself except as a locus, a theoretical locus, of a multitude of experiences. He speaks of a thousand things, and pretends he is nobody. He is *zersplittert,* broken into innumerable fragments and objectified even to himself. The atom of the soul too is smashed. The soul has disappeared and the human being is a thing of such devastation as no building up is able to restore into grace and stability.

The new infinite is made up of an infinite fragmentation of the old eternal. The invisible dome of the eternal is fallen down and shattered into an infinity of colorful pieces, and the people are turned into a race of junk-men. There they are, the fragments, in an infinite variety of sizes, shapes and colors, hiding the heavens and the sun. See the men rushing about, filling their bags with the stuff and running home in order to hoard it. "See how many there are," say the men with the wild eyes and the hooked fingers, "piles and piles of the thing. There never were so many things before. We will find more and more as we go along. We shall be busy picking up and enjoying all our days. We shall make new things out of them, and those who come after us will carry on where we leave off. Now we have something exciting and useful to do. We have something to look forward to; something we can call our own and enjoy. Some day there will be more, enough for everybody. We shall all be rich. We shall no longer quarrel. And there shall be peace, and we shall be happy at last; not we, of course, but those who come after us. Today we must pick up and if necessary fight for the pickings. But some day the fighting shall be over, and there shall only be picking and filling the bag." Drink, gentlemen, to the Timeless Pluriverse of Infinite Picking!

When man is detemporalized, he lives as though he did not die, and thus the most devastating of all lies, the lie of the irrelevance of death to life, is born and begins its idiotic career of rape and immolation. The fragmented spirit loses its soul. Death masquerades as life and life becomes macabre. Indeed, there is music, laughter and lust. But, there is death in the air and consternation with forebodings of doom. Dead spirits must live in apprehension even while they have no fear of death, and they must destroy one another in despair of they know not what.

Truly, a marvellous thing has happened. Even the lovers of mankind no longer care about men and women. Heaven knows, everybody is humanitarian. Everybody is working for peace and prosperity. Statesmen, preachers, professors, capitalists, communists, socialists; farmers, workers, indutrialists; idealists, realists, and pragmatists: they all are working for the benefit of mankind, not only for the present but also for a prolonged and dim future. They all seek freedom and justice for all men. They are working hard toward the elimination of pain and drudgery and toward the greatest pleasure of the greatest number. But, their indiscriminate concern for persons and things, their willingness to sacrifice people for the sake of abstractions, their strange failures to accomplish the good they propose, the surprising ways in which they seek peace but multiply trouble,—these things more than indicate that they themselves are the victims of the fragmentation of man which is playing havoc with the peoples of our time. Hence they continue to fail, and our latter end is worse than the former. The repudiation of personal existence and the miseries of men go together, and it is absurd to expect a blessed life while we nullify the human being who is the only possible bearer of it.

5. *THE ORIGINS OF THE VICES: OF UNREASON*

There might be a pursuit of goods purely for the sake of pleasure one expects from them. Such pursuit would be guided and regulated by reason. Reason would calculate the amount of pleasure in view and direct the will to follow it with proportionate zeal. It would control ambition and measure out the emotions according to the anticipated good. Its calculus would not be perfect; but still, it would maintain some proportion between desire and its object. The more would appear as more and the less as less. Things would be more or less good and they would afford more or less pleasure. Emotion would correspond to idea and the heart would follow the mind. And throughout, having would have nothing to do with being. Were being irrelevant to having, there would be neither unreason, nor lust, nor despair nor any absolute passion. And having would be free from the grasping and avarice among men.

Lust, avarice, sensuality, pride, ambition, despair, violence, and all inordinations in men's behavior, more or less obvious everywhere, arise from the confusion of being with having in all human existence. Irrationality as distinct from deficiency in reasoning, lust as other than desire, avarice as it differs from "self-love," sensuality as against sensibility, pride which corrupts self-respect, ambition without a rational end, despair which overwhelms legitimate hope, impetuosity and violence posing as zeal, etc.—all these, in principle, are rooted not in impulses for having but in the anticipated victory of nonbeing over being. It is the despair of life and not the hope of gain that is the prior source of human vice.

The vices have a mysterious power before which our reason succumbs, day in and day out. Everyone will acknowledge that our vices are irrational. Selfishness, acting as though the good of another were negligible, is unintelligent. Pride, estimating oneself as greater than one is in fact, is a perversion of reason. Ill will, the sheer desire to hurt another, is dangerous stupidity. Everyone knows that these vices are contrary to reason, and everyone succumbs to them in spite of reason.

The usual explanations of unreason are circular. Why do men act irrationally, that is, why are their responses incongruous with the facts which evoke them? Because their emotions are aroused. Why are their emotions aroused? Because they are afraid or angry. Why are they afraid or angry, that is, unjustly afraid or angry? Because they are irrational. A complete circle, well drawn indeed, but leading nowhere. It is easy enough to observe that men become emotional and "lose their heads." But it is not so easy to see why they react to the finite as though it were infinite, which is the root of unreason. The virtual absoluteness of greed, pride, ill will, finds no explanation in one's relations to the finite objects in one's environment. There is no explaining the "power of the emotions" in relation to finite goods and evils.

The power of the emotions is the power of life in recoil from finitude and bursting upon a finite good or evil. It is the absolute power of being hurled upon having and not having. The emotions overcome reason because their power is drawn from being itself. The discriminations of reason expose one to the relative power of some finite good. The indiscriminating impetuosity of the emotions is derived from the absolute contradiction between being and nonbeing. Hence, a constant tendency to violate reason, to embrace evil rather than good, death rather than life, is integral to human existence and ensues in the perennial surprises of destructive activity. It is not the race's lack in reasoning power but the race's subjection to the power of death that makes our common existence the evil producing thing that it is.

The dominion of selfishness over the human spirit is exercised with the power of being confronted with nonbeing. Life confronted with death is absolutely impetuous, and exercises its impetuosity against other life. The impulse to survive is informed with the absolute energy of the will to live. Thus a man seeks to survive another as though survival meant the victory of life over death. Thus also, the means of survival, which are a matter of having, are sought after as though they were the means of "eternal life."

The selfish will to have is endowed with an impulse incommensurate with its several objectives. When I try to get hold of something rather than let another man have it, I am driven by an impulse which has no proportion to the good in sight. When I want anything I want it as though it were a matter of life and death. I am absolutely gratified when I get it, and absolutely frustrated when I do not get it. Besides, I am not so very happy when the other man gets the same thing. I want more than he has, no matter how much we both may have. I want to be superior to him even if my superiority gives me no palpable advantage in possession and security in possession. As I want absolutely to survive, I want absolutely to be superior. I want to have more than he has, not because this more is necessary for my happiness as dictated by need, but because the fact itself of having more makes me happy.

Selfishness is born of the delusion that to survive is to overcome death and that acquisition is justified by the impulse for survival. Selfishness is a giddiness in the midst of this double delusion and its natural outcomes are unreason and common misery.

Pride is the consequence of a similar distortion. You are superior to another in wealth, culture, intelligence, skill, manners and virtue. Well and good. There should be no harm in your knowing it. That is rational, just and edifying. It will encourage proper self-respect and present you with your duty as a superior man. But why your contempt? Why must you absolutize your superiority and his inferiority? Why must you be blind to your shortcoming and blind also to some little virtue in him? Why this, "I am good and you are no good; I am clever, you are dumb; I am rich, you are poor; I am cultivated, you are uncouth; I am high, you are low?" It is characteristic of pride that it will admit of no degrees. The proud man is superior simply considered. That other man is inferior simply considered. The superior man will either ignore the inferior man, or patronize him, or insult him, or simply use him. But he will not respect him. He simply cannot give the other man his due. Now, obviously such pride is irrational. And strangely enough it is more frequent among the clever and successful than among "the dumb ones who never get very far." Pride goes with an incapacity for just comparison; but it does not come from poor reason. It comes from an overthrow of reason by a power greater than itself, the power of life met with death. The absolute contradiction between being and nonbeing absolutizes the relativities of having and not having, and pride is born in the process.

Despair, the opposite of pride, is similarly constituted.

What is there to despair about? Is it not true that "while there is life there is hope"? You cannot have everything. But you can have something. You cannot do everything you please, but you can do something. You may not become the greatest and the best, but you can be greater and do better. So long as you are not dead you are somebody and there is some hope of improvement. Why then do you despair? Why this, "I have hit bottom; there is no hope for me; I have nothing, I shall never have anything? I wish I were dead"? We know you are having a hard time. Life has become very complicated and there is a constant stream of annoyances. Very well. You should be somewhat unhappy. Perhaps you should be very unhappy. That is sensible. But why despair? There is no answer to this question in terms of having and not having, that is, according to reason. Nevertheless, there is despair and it is destroying a soul. Whence is it? Listen closely to the despairing man: "I am through. I am done for. I am lost. There is no hope. It is finished." The man has lost fortune, or his good name, or his job. And now, *he* is through, *he* is done for, *he* is lost; *it, everything,* is finished. This despair is not a matter of having and not having; it comes from being itself. The despairing man has one life to live. He must now have what he wants, or he may never have it. Now he must have it. Now he does not have it. He shall never have it. There is no hope. Nonbeing energizes not having into an absolute, and the consequence is despair.

Thus it is that not being and not having work on each other. Being despairs before nonbeing. Its despair absolutizes not having. Not having itself evokes the despair in nonbeing which in turn makes not having into sheer emptiness. The world goes black and life is virtually ended. But life is not ended. Therefore, there is a recoil from desperation into pride. "Did I say I have nothing? I have everything, everything worth having. It is you who have nothing, nothing I would give twopence for. By my wisdom, I am greater with the little I have, than you are with your great wealth and power. You have much, but I am great. My nothing is everything, and your everything is nothing. . . ." Thus our having and not having, impregnated with our being and nonbeing, become continual sources of at once pride and despair.

The same applies to gluttony. Some food is tasty and some more tasty. Tasty food should be enjoyed and more tasty food should be enjoyed more. But, tasty food is eaten as though it were absolutely delicious and less tasty food is rejected with curses and woeful frustration. Even behind a decorous exterior, men go at their food with a passion which is overwhelming. They develop exotic tastes and are gratified when they spend a small fortune on their bellies. There is no limit to the refinement of their tastes and to the piquancy of their enjoyment through nose and palate. Their physical need for food and drink is greatly outdone by a spiritual need for sensual enjoyment, and the hunger of the body is replaced by a need for absolute pleasure. People eat food as though it were the "medicine of immortality," with a straining after some absolute which is, in this instance, sensuality. Sensuality, *gourmandize,* gluttony, the urge to eat the tastiest of foods and to eat it indefinitely, are inexplicable except as expressions of an ultimate anxiety concerning life itself. Because eating is necessary in order to maintain life, it is corrupted easily with being's horror of nonbeing. Men eat and drink as though their eating and drinking meant the triumph of life over death. Gluttony is another transmutation of the love of being for being. If men did not die, neither would they glut. Angels never glut. It is in man that the appetite for food is changed to lust for it and men will risk death for a better dish.

The same is true of human sexuality which has become the problem of problems. This means of procreation, which is as natural as eating and drinking, has become a prime source of human confusion and misery. Some think it explains every deviltry in the world. This may be going quite too far. But there is no question that there is neither rhyme nor reason to human sexuality. Here again one observes a "concupiscence," a relentlessness, a preoccupation, a repudiation of times and seasons, a sheer disregard for reason and consideration, an absolutizing passion, which are inexplicable in terms of nature. The cunning, the selfishness, the envies and hatreds, the domination and abuse, and even murders, which go with human love making, suggest the diversion of an absolute passion into the sexual function. The procreating act is endowed with the absolute energy of the creative act in all being as against non-being. It is done as though it meant a victory of life over death. In "love" it is that human finitude is forgotten most effectively. It is also there that melancholy becomes the most authentic foretaste of death. The ecstasy and dread in love have their energy from the power of death.

The same is true of all human vices; for instance, envy. Someone is richer, healthier, wiser, more famous than you are. You wish you also could be healthier, wealthier, etc. That is natural. That is rational. But why the strange bitterness in your envy? Why do you envy him, not more or less, but absolutely? Why do you shamefully or shamelessly wish he were in the poor house, or in prison, or dead? Human envy is deadly even when its occasion is trivial, and is restrained mainly by fear.

Defeat and humiliation at the hands of another arouse the imagination to visions of some devastating blow which shall crush the evil doer utterly and once for all. The insulted and injured go about sour and listless until the offender be repaid "seventy times seven" or kind nature dissipate the memory of the offense suffered. Even accidental evil evokes a response which is virtually murderous. That is why people are taught to say "I am sorry" after the most trivial and unpremeditated giving of offense to anyone whatsoever. This social convention is a tribute to the unpredictable irascibility of men and to the sheer incongruity between harm suffered and evil proposed. Multitudes in the world are destroyed violently for reasons which do not call for more than a rebuke. Every other man who feels powerful enough will pay back ten times for every damage he suffers. He will suddenly discover his honor and go out to defend it in the midst of wreck and ruin. His honor conceals the obvious extravagance of the vengeance he intends, and justifies his irrational response to evil done or even expected. Every evil instance acts as an occasion for the quickening of a metaphysical distemper of his being, and a signal for an encounter with death.

Failure and the threat of failure in the pursuit of goods and pleasure arouse men to hostility and consequent deeds which have little bearing upon any rational purpose. Men become enemies not because enmity can do away with its occasion but because they are already desperate about their existence. Enmity which wills the death of another has no objective cause. There is no evil commensurate with death and no source of murderous intention outside the would-be murderer. Goods and life are utterly disproportionate, and murder for goods is contrary to reason. Hence, that men will murder for goods is evidence that goods are invested with the value of life, that in seeking goods men are seeking for a life beyond death. This is the reason for the murder in the mind of a man whom another has deprived of his possessions. This is why men want absolute power which shall make them absolutely secure with their possessions. This is why they have perennially put up with tyranny for the sake of security with their possessions.

Possessions are not merely goods to be enjoyed. They are counterfeits of life. This is why men want goods more than a long life. Goods are endowed with the absolute goodness of life itself, while our finite life is considered an ambiguous and most doubtful good. Hence men cling to goods with a passion which is infinite, and frustration in the pursuit of goods makes life itself worthless. Hence the deadly vices in our common life are inspired by the pursuit of goods and not by the love of life. The vicious care nothing for life. But they care absolutely for goods. When they have goods, they forget life. When they lose goods, they hate life. Goods are their life and for the sake of goods, which is their life, they exploit, oppress, envy, hate, and even murder.

The vanity of possessions is a recurrent theme among the wise men of the race. It is an open secret even among the worldlings that goods and the Good never coincide. Men are unhappy with what they have, but they are loath to admit the fact to themselves and to others because they shun the despair in such an admission. They pursue goods with a hectic zeal, in the desperate hope that sometime and somehow they will thus attain the Good. But since they know this hope to be vain, they will argue that the pursuit itself is the Good or that their hope will be realized at some distant time after they are dead. Thus they justify their unreason with their religion of Progress, and live and die in their despair. In this despair they cease to be men and do evil.

6. *POWER FOR GOOD AND GOODS FOR POWER*

There is no possession without frustration. Power spent for goods does not yield the good we seek in them. There is a radical incongruity between power used and good attained, and this incongruity makes the use of power irrational. Hence, power alone, of all goods in man's power, is a good congruous with itself; and in all use of power by men there is a pursuit of power for its own sake. The frustration of power in the pursuit of goods turns power itself into the good. Despair concerning the good turns power toward itself as the only certain good, so that, in possessing, one is never certain whether the thing possessed or the possessing itself is the good. It is no longer clear whether the good is for the sake of power or the power is for the sake of the good. Everything is possessed as much for the sake of possessing as for the sake of the good in it. The pleasure in having becomes inseparable from the pleasure in enjoying, and enjoyment is subordinated to the pursuit of power. Now power itself is pursued as its own ultimate end. It is enjoyed as license with both things and people. There is now an absolute gratification in power and action by fiat. Through the alchemy of despair with goods, power which is for the sake of the good becomes itself the good. The means becomes the end and the poison of unreason is injected into the roots of human existence. The resultant confusion of the human mind is chaotic.

Since by nature and reason, power is for the sake of life and enjoyment, reason must always try to justify the use of it in terms of some good. Power means the ability to do something, and without power you cannot do anything. You cannot even keep alive. Power is the condition of all good and the more power you have the more good you can actualize both for yourself and for others. Hence, it is obvious that the pursuit of power is natural, rational and right. Hence there is a perpetual green light on the road to power. On the other hand, everybody knows that this same road is strewn all over, on both sides, before, after, and under, with the corpses of life, health, liberty, goods, peace, pleasure, and all the ends for which the road and the vehicle both are supposed to have been built. Goods are foregone and men murdered, for the sake of some great good at some future time. There is presumably some greatest good which is worth all the dreadful miseries attendant upon the pursuit of power at any given time. And some men are full of such magnificent gas that they take off from the road altogether, willing to crash down en route to eutopia which everyone agrees means nowhere at all. When these aerialists get going, not only the road but also the surrounding country is strewn with the mangled and dismembered. Power is for the sake of the good, but the good is being continually destroyed for the sake of some greater good. And what is this greater good? Who has seen and handled and smelled it? What makes it greater than the goods which are thrown away for its sake at this time? What makes it better than health, peace, freedom, and concord among men? What is this good for the sake of which men lose their minds, their friends, their families, their goods, and even their lives? There is no such good. The whole thing is a lie. The Good for the sake of which men seek continually to augment their power, power over their fellowmen, is a product of mad imagination. It is a disguise for power and the pursuit of it is a covering for lust.

It is lust for power generated by the despair of life with goods that drives men to the basic unreason of destroying goods while they lust after them, of killing one another in their search for life. Incredible as it may seem, power is become more valuable than life. Power supplies the glory in possession and the sweetness in enjoyment. There is no human good, including the love of men and women, that does not derive its filling quality from the power that comes with it. The vanity of all things makes power the good which men seek in all goods. It is power and not goods alone that makes the chest to expand and the heart to be satisfied.

It is better to be a man of maximum power and moderate possessions than to have much goods with little power. This superiority of power to goods is due partly to the security attained through power and partly to the prospects of more goods through power. But the fact remains that men jeopardize both goods and security for the sake of power. Besides, security and riches are themselves incentives towards domination. The man who is secure lacks the fear which discourages wilfulness, and the wealthy man loves to lord it over his fellowmen. Powerful men find their self-realization not in their security and not in their goods, but in their lordship.

The reason for this mysterious preference is as follows. The connection between life and any good whatsoever is incidental. Besides, no good, not even food and drink, can alter a man's situation in relation to death. To survive one's neighbor is not the same as to survive death. Hence, no good can pretend to be a valid substitute for one's being alive. The relationship between life and power is different. There is no being without power, and also no acting without it. We become aware of our existence in our actions, and our actions are the expressions of our power. Being and power are so bound together that they constitute the two primary modes of our existence. Hence it is that power assumes readily the absoluteness of existence itself, and is preferred as a good beside which no other good, including survival itself, is good enough. When a man wields power, he affirms his existence, and his soul is satisfied.

The shadow of one's non-existence darkens all the goods he enjoys. Goods are temporal and act as tokens of our own temporality. We are always anxious about our goods, and our anxiety about them quickens the primary anxiety of our life confronted with death or our nonbeing. Power sought and enjoyed for its own sake is nontemporal. In wielding power, a man becomes oblivious to his lifetime. Power goes out of him without any end or purpose. It has no relation to any good, past, present, or future. It has no relevance to the passage of time, or even to time itself. In the act of mastery, a man is lifted above the world of change and mortality. The moment of the exercise of power becomes an instance of absolute being.

The seduction in the implicit logic of lust for power is obvious when we consider that power is no substitute for life. Without life there is no power, and no power can remove the anxiety of life. The lords and princes among men shall die. They shall die even as the weakest and the poorest of men. Their power is absolutely powerless with regard to death, and their mastery shall in no way alter their fate. Even if they make the thousands to march at their bidding and the ten thousands to fall down at their word, one day they shall neither live nor rule in the land of the living. No man can with his power change his dying life into a life without death. Life and power are not commensurate one with the other. It is madness to imagine that power is the Life and the Good. And no one would imagine such a thing were it not for the despair of men in "the valley of the shadow of death."

Where there is despair of being, the love of power as a means is turned into a lust for power as an end in itself. The power with which a being maintains itself according to its nature is turned into a power absurdly indifferent to being without which there is neither power nor any good. Thus the lust for power emerges as the prime unreason in human life and bedevils the whole existence of man.

No amount of power can change being's being in relation to nonbeing, or remove the dread in human existence. Power rather establishes dread and much power turns it into a panic. This is why the more powerful men are, the more dangerous they are. This is why men of power are exposed to arbitrary and irrational action which lets loose torrents of devastating evil. There is no telling when they will make a "mistake" which will mean wholesale misery and even death. Great men or men of power are men who are "at their rope's end." Power is the last substitute for life which can be proposed in this world. There is nothing beyond sheer mastery to which a man can aspire, nothing except "eternal life." If mastery itself cannot overcome the dread in man, there is nothing on earth to which a man can turn. The last hope of man dies with the frustration which attends mastery. Now despair operates with full force and becomes at once murderous and suicidal. The greater the man, the more ready he is to sacrifice his fellowmen toward one end or another, and the more contempt he has for "mere survival." In fact, contempt for life is the great man's convincing evidence of his greatness and the measure of his true difference from the little men whom he dominates. Lesser men seek security, pleasure, a good name, and the rest. The great man knows the vanity of these things. He knows in his bones that the only possibility of self-realization is in power. Hence, he will jeopardize all things for the sake of power. Such temper of mind is unintelligible except as an act of desperation, and the despair in it arises from the essential emptiness of power as an object of lust. It must not be forgotten, moreover, that the seeds of greatness are in all men.

CHAPTER IV

Lust for Freedom

1. *THE PERIL IN PRUDENCE*

THE THOROUGH DEPENDENCE of men one upon another in the pursuit of goods is a constant threat to their existence as persons. In the captivating procession of goods and the experiences of goods, the human being concerned with his destiny becomes a matter of indifference, an absurdity which cannot be fitted into any rational system of ideas. His place is taken by the prudent man who immerses himself in his environment of men and machines, adjusts himself to the institutions around him, and gives himself up to a life of acquisition. The reasonable man confronted with the powers in modern society yields to them and sets out to control them for his own benefit. But in yielding or in dominating he is no longer free. His very reason which is by nature the means of his freedom becomes the chief instrument of his bondage and is secretly recognized as his own chief enemy.

But there is a constant revulsion against prudence. A man is repeatedly moved to do "as he pleases," that is, to push reason aside and to follow an impulse to act by fiat. He cannot call anything his own unless he may do what he pleases with it. No power he has is truly his unless he can use it wilfully. The more power he has, the more he is driven to have his way simply because it is his way. And when his power is great, nobody can tell him what to do. In an industrial society where men acquire goods and power in constant and absolute dependence upon other men, the freedom to do as one pleases is very highly prized. In fact, there seems to be nothing so precious as one's ability to do as one pleases. Men at times risk both goods and power for the sake of doing as they will.

Men are, as individuals, often too prudent to "act free"; hence, they form groups which assume the impudence to defy both law and reason. As members of some organization, they enjoy a freedom of action which would be scandalous in individual citizens. Such freedom to do as they please, finds its ultimate expression in the sovereign nation which can do no wrong. The sovereign nation is the State and the State is the final projection of men's irresistible desire to do as they please. The willingness of men to die in order to preserve the sovereignty of the State is utterly inexplicable except as an expression of wilfulness which cannot be satisfied otherwise. The deeper the bondage of men in society, the more jealous they are for the sovereignty of a fictitious State.

Lust for freedom is today at once concealed and energized by lust for machine-made goods. Even the traditional freedoms of a democratic society are now plainly instrumental to the accumulation and enjoyment of goods. The free man today is one who suffers no interference in his pursuit of the goods around him. He is free from want, that is, he has what he wants. He is free from fear, that is, he is not afraid that he will be hindered from making money and keeping it. His other freedoms, the freedom of speech, of assembly, of the press, of religion, of trial by jury, are, in the last analysis, symbolic of the great freedoms of acquisition and enjoyment.

An essential element in the blessedness of having money is that one can spend it as one pleases. In spite of every rational objection, every one is deeply convinced that what he has is absolutely his own; that outside interference with it must be accepted at best as a necessary evil; that to own it is the same as to be able to do what he pleases with it. To realize that other men have a say about what he is to do with his own is to spoil both his ownership of it and his satisfaction in it.

Like imposing one's will upon another, doing something merely because one has willed to do it is absolutely gratifying.

A good attained in spite of one's will is not a consummatory. good. It is flat, as though its very goodness had been wrung out of it. Freedom is the good of the good, so that even where evil and not good is attained, to do as one pleases is, absolutely speaking, good. Lust makes power itself good. So, lust makes freedom itself good.

The price of welfare through prudence is the objectification of the self. The prudent man is a locus of objectives. His selfhood is dissipated by hungers and their satisfactions. He is a seat of a succession of pain and pleasure, and exists preoccupied in removing the former and in increasing the latter. The causes of pain and pleasure are themselves causes and effects and belong to a nexus of causation which is the objective world. The prudent man himself, concerned with pain and pleasure, is a cause and effect in the same nexus. He has no freedom over against his objectives. Or, if he have such freedom, he does not care to exercise it. Thus, the self, which is the seat of freedom, is repudiated and made to keep silent.

The man of prudence loses sight of the radical opposition between being and nonbeing in himself. Thus he loses his soul. He rejects life and tastes of death. Nonbeing acts as the very form of his own existence, and he no longer cares to oppose it. His humanity is abrogated, and his love turns into lust.

The impulse to do as one pleases without regard to reason or purpose is a panicky self-assertion. The suspension of reason by the emotions has its source in a heaving effort of the self to break the bonds of the world of things which threaten his strangulation. Men are constantly tempted to drown out the voice of reason not because they "get excited" but because they want to remember they are alive and not dead. "Excitement" is an effect before it is a cause. There is a constant temptation to rebel against reason, to consign prudence to the devil, to repudiate duty and obligation, to nullify the "will power" of men around us. There is no telling when a man or a woman is going to break loose and do as he or she well pleases. There is no telling when someone is going to get excited and lose his head. There is no telling just how much or how little will make a man do something as ruinous as absurd.

If a man manages to keep his temper too often and for too long, he may be called a good man but he himself wonders if he be not a good corpse instead. It seems to be simply and universally necessary that an ordinary human being, at some time or another, for a good reason or poor, rise up to his full height and say, "No! I shall not do as you say. I shall not do as any one says. You can do your worst. I will not do as you will. I will do as *I* please." The very thought that sometime or other, one might have the courage to stand up and speak like this, has in it a metaphysical thrill which is never found in the voice of prudence. Listen to the prudent man: "Oh yes, certainly. I agree. What you say is very reasonable. We will both profit from the course you propose. Thank you very much." Such speech is of course decent, sensible, profitable, and all that. But also, it is infernally dull. There is something cheap and almost shameful about it. One cannot go on talking like that, day in and day out, with every shopkeeper of a man that comes along, without losing one's self respect and without wondering if one be still alive. For very life's sake, one day a man must tell the oily fellow that he will not play the game. He must throw prudence to the winds and assert his selfhood by doing something not because it is good for him, but because, simply because, he was willed to do it. Such a deed has in it a gratification, and even an ecstasy, which come from the depths of the human soul and return into the depths bearing a counterfeit of the joy of life itself. To be, to be the being one is, is absolutely good. There is no good which can replace it. Hence, men in bondage to goods and to their fellowmen for the sake of goods, cannot live without the freedom to do as they please, purely because they please to will to do what they do. Lust for freedom is the unfree man's futile bid for regaining his lost selfhood. It is self-assertion without selfhood, for no man can live as a self without the use of his reason. The self evoked by lust is an imposter, and the thrill that comes from doing as one will cannot but end in despair.

2. *FREEDOM AS ARBITRARY WILL*

As there is a love of power for the sake of survival, peace, security, etc., so there is a love of freedom for the sake of realizing some good proposed by reason. Freedom is the exercise of one's ability to make a living, to buy a house, to marry and beget children, to enjoy goods and the society of men. Freedom, like power, is for something, for something good. In general, one is free when there is no interference with one's pursuit of a good. Such freedom is good as a means to a good end and it is at once rational and natural.

Lust for freedom is something altogether different. It is generated by despair with destiny, and with every rational good. It is a radical repudiation of freedom for the good. Doing as we will pleases us because every good we pursue and obtain turns out to be not good enough. The lust for freedom is a desperate effort to find the good in nothing at all. When it becomes evident that the good we receive is not the good we seek, we are left with the illusory possibility that the seeking itself is the good. It is now pretended that it is fun to look for a treasure even though we know that there is no treasure to find. It is now insisted that the treasure is the looking for one that does not exist. It becomes a matter of common agreement and religious zeal that every one has an inviolable right to pursue a happiness which consists in the pursuit of nothing. Everybody must be free to pursue. Everybody must be free to pursue as he will or as it pleases him. He must not allow either mind or feelings to dictate his course of action. He certainly must not be constrained to act according to the interests of his neighbors. Not even he himself, as a man among men, must be allowed to dictate to himself what he shall or shall not do. He must be free over against all being including his own. He must be free over against all nature and law of nature including his own. He must be free to act as moved in relation to nothing. A man, therefore, is free when he regards his essence as nonbeing (*sic!*); when he who is nonbeing acts according to a will which is nothing; when he can bring himself to thumb his nose at being and every good entertained by his mind. Lust for freedom is a repudiation of being and order and good. It is the essence of nihilism; the freedom for life turned into a freedom for death, nonbeing activated by dread and despair.

By lust for freedom, men enslave one another and oppress one another; by it, homes are turned into hell, associations fall apart, societies disintegrate, nations are sacrificed and their cultures destroyed. This is the lust which fills the world with agony of death and makes the people to die even as they live. Lust for freedom is born of the anticipation of death as the only end of bondage and despair. Hence it is a lust for freedom in death, anticipated by a destroying freedom, a freedom which is not enjoyed except in disregard for reason and its love of life and happiness.

The energy of lust for freedom is the energy of life itself. Hence it is that inhumanities and destructions occur and recur at any time and at any place where men live together. Men violate one another and fill the world with woe as though driven by a power which overwhelms their good sense and will to live. The voice of prudence even when loudest sounds hollow, whereas the secret whisperings of self-assertion entice men to madness and common misery. Such irresistible and world-encompassing power in lust for freedom can be none other than the energy of being diverted by dread and despair. There is much too much cruelty in this world. And it can only be the exuberance of life turned into a dance of death.

Lust for freedom is the perversion of nature. A man's love for being, his use of reason for his own ends, reason's use of power towards being and good—these are natural. On the contrary, a freedom over against reason is contrary to nature. And since there is nothing contrary to nature that is not a perversion of it, it follows that lust for freedom is the perversion of a being's love for being; that is, it is a hatred of being, an impulse to destroy one's being. It is the power of life changed into a power toward death. Hence it destroys as universally and effectively as life itself creates and builds up. Love and lust, nature and its corruption, good and evil are locked up together in a deadly conflict whose ultimate outcome seems to be death.

Each man lives in two kingdoms at once, and these two are in conflict within himself. The mind works in relation to both being and nonbeing. In relation to being, the mind is the seat of prudence and common sense. In relation to nonbeing, it is the seat of despair and lust for freedom. In both relations, it generates emotion. In relation to being, the mind generates love. In relation to nonbeing it generates lust. Thus love is opposed to lust and the mind becomes the scene of relentless warfare between love and lust. In this warfare, lust is stronger than love because no earthly good can remove the despair in man. Hence the most cultivated mind cannot be depended upon to be consistently rational, especially in the face of some evil which agitates its despair. And certainly, unless there be some way of dealing with men's despair, it is absurd to hope that some day a sufficient number of minds will be sufficiently cultivated to turn the chaos of our social existence into one of order and a common good.

Torn between love and lust, a man's life becomes a contradiction. He seeks the good and ends in evil. He prizes reason and follows unreason. He pursues power and ends in powerlessness. He yearns for freedom and ends in bondage. The more a man can have his way, the nearer he comes to pushing himself out of the way. He negates himself even as he asserts himself. He pursues death even while he is anxious for his life, for what he shall eat and what he shall drink and wherewith he shall be clothed. And he covers his unreason with his lust, his will to die with his wilfulness. When the soul and its freedom are repudiated, there appears the "ego" which is a seat of a lust for freedom. And this lust is prized and cherished above all else, even while its last end is death.

Anyone who goes out to promote the good life in terms of

peace, prosperity and the like must reckon with the fact that to do as one will is sweeter than both peace and many goods. He should not be surprised and left helpless when his best laid plans for the common good are frustrated by apparently sane and sensible people. He should rather recognize that so long as the lust in man is ignored and thus allowed a free course through his body and soul alike, the social system will continue to become infected by a virulent poison which shall give us chills and fevers in spite of all the medicaments on hand.

Lust for power is the primary transmutation of the love of being. But few men are able to be sufficiently powerful to entertain the delusion of omnipotence without making obvious fools of themselves. Usually, the real choice is between freedom and unfreedom, between doing and not doing as one will. If I cannot dominate another person, I can try to keep him from dominating me. It is better to be a master than to be free, and better to be free than to be a slave. Of course, the more power one has, the more one can do as one pleases. One, therefore, seeks power in order that one may do as one pleases. But, there is not much good in doing as one pleases without asserting power over one's fellowmen. Thus, lust for freedom and lust for power coalesce and men lust for power as they lust for freedom. Lust for power is disguised as the love of freedom, and "free men" show a strong impulse to lord it over their fellowmen.

CHAPTER V

Guilt in the Career of Lust

1. *THE BITTERNESS IN LUST*

A STRANGE BITTERNESS attends the lust for power. The man of lust dominates his neighbor without the joy which accompanies a natural use of power. He is cast down even while he humbles those around him. His humanity is balked within him. His understanding and compassion alike become inactive and his very soul becomes numb in the cold fire of his lust. He can neither give love nor receive it, and this frustration of nature leaves him indifferent both to life and to good.

The bitterness in the man of lust grows out of the violation of nature, his own and that of his neighbor. This violation is wrong and makes him guilty. It is this wrong and the guilt of it that make for the peculiar and devastating bitterness in human lust.

The victim of lust is overcome by a corresponding bitterness. His pain at being lorded over is unlike any other evil he suffers. It arouses in him a peculiar resentment and effects in him a unique frustration. This particular evil is an insult as well as an injury. It is a violation of his nature, a repudiation of his humanity, a blow struck not at his body but at his soul. The man of lust ignores his victim as a rational and responsible being. He overlooks his hopes and anxieties. He cares nothing for his destiny, nothing for the dread of the void in the human soul, nothing for the love which comforts the soul in its despair of life and good alike. Lust is the essential treachery of one man toward another. It is an unnatural and unjustifiable breaking of the bond of a common life in which men may pursue their

85

common and several goods. It is a wilful assault upon personal existence. Hence its victim is subjected to a unique ignominy. His soul becomes the seat of peculiar desolation in which self-respect, trust, goodwill, generosity, and all the healthy plants of human nature, wither away, and their withering signifies the death of the soul itself. There is no overlooking the wanton treachery in lust. Lust is an irrational and therefore inexplicable violation of humanity; and, both because it is treacherous and because it is inhuman, it is guilty, both in essence and in its works.

The bitterness of the victim of lust is evoked by his own guilt. An innocent man would not become bitter. After all, the lust of another cannot in fact destroy his soul. It can neither abrogate his humanity nor cause his love to die within him. Innocence has no power over pain; but it is omnipotent against guilt. Guilt alone responds to guilt in bitterness. One who chafes under the tyranny of another is himself a potential tyrant. He cannot claim immunity to the lust causing him to lose his joy. He knows that the lust in the tyrant is, to say the least, inflamed by the guilty lust within him. He himself has more than once aroused others to wilfulness and will to power by his own impulse to lord it over them. Even now that he is helpless, he is not unwilling to see the situation reversed and to find himself able to lord it over his domineering neighbor. His plea of innocence is hollow. His self-pity is hardly in good taste. He may, in any given instance, be the victim of another's lust. But, he has not been always innocent. Not having been always innocent, he is capable of lust. There is lust in him, and with it also guilt. The lust of his enemy energizes his own lust, and the guilt of the other confirms the guilt in him. The bitterness in his soul is the joint product of these two guilts. The power of the other's guilt is derived from the power of his own guilt; the desolation in his soul is wrought by the mysterious guilt attached to his existence in despair.

There are two universal characteristics of "human nature" which indicate guilt as integral to human existence. One is our strange incapacity for joy and the other is a common repudiation of guilt. Everyone is innocent, and everyone is without joy unless he have its counterfeit known as pleasure. But, how can one be without guilt and also without joy? Joy is nothing else than the first fruit of integrity. It is the product of life according to nature. Every being has joy in so far as it exists in the exercise of its natural powers and in fulfilment of its proper end. In human beings, there can be joy only where there is love, a common life in which every man pursues and attains the good according to his reason..The lack of joy among us means nothing other than that we do not exist in love, or that ours is a life of lust and guilt. Hence it is that everyone is looking for joy and few are they who find it.

Everyone is innocent in his own eyes, and yet no one is surprised by inhumanity and even by the cruelties in our world. In spite of every conspiracy of silence, no one doubts that his neighbor is quite capable of a guilty act, or that he exists in guilt. No one can, moreover, convince his own soul, leave alone his neighbor, that he himself is incapable of a guilty act, or that he exists in innocence. But to exist in guilt is intolerable. It means the absence of integrity, and with it the ruin of our nature, which is death. Hence, everybody is continually justifying himself—but alas, there is no joy in this business because we are in fact guilty, and no evasion or repudiation of guilt can change our existence. Guilt disavowed is only guilt covered up. But guilt covered up loses none of its power and becomes all the more irresistible in its career of lust and destruction. The misery of our common life today is inescapable evidence that we exist in guilt, and that unless our existence is altered we shall see neither peace nor good.

2. *GUILT WITHOUT GOD*

There is a common opinion that "the twilight of the gods" has meant also the twilight of conscience. The sense of guilt used to be active in the presence of a just and all-seeing God who is able to reward man according to his deserts. Violent excitations of conscience went with the belief that an offended Deity was wroth and ready to perpetrate some dire calamity. The sense of guilt had mixed with it dismal fear of dryness, blight, disease, pestilence, hunger and death. Men living in absolute dependence upon nature's God alternated between profound gratitude and terrible fear. It was natural and rational that they should have lived under His "moral law," acknowledging their duty of obedience to Him and fearful in their repeated and guilty disobedience.

But now, it is man we must fear, and not nature and its God or gods. What causes millions of men, women and children today to suffer from cold, hunger and starvation? Other men. How is it that multitudes are diseased and demoralized, without peace, security, hope, and joy? Because of other men. When men today become distracted with forebodings of evil, and become mad and run toward disaster, what makes them do it? Their neighbors. A has lost his home; B his job; C his health; D his mind. E is dead. How did all this happen? Well, A's bank has failed; B happened to insult his boss; C worried about his family; D lost his two sons. E was killed by a truck and in the truck was a man talking to another man. The more power man has over nature and the more he improves upon her works, the less he fears her and the far less he is concerned with the God of nature. On the other hand, the more he is dependent upon his fellowmen, the more he lives in the fear of them. We have achieved a new dependence upon our fellowmen, and our whole perspective upon existence is changed.

The man in an environment of men and machines is almost instinctively a "moral relativist." He worries about right and wrong only in relation to his fellowmen. What they call right he also calls right; what they call wrong, he also calls wrong. The sting in wrong is in the evil consequences which may follow from it. The less he suffers from wrongdoing, the less guilty he feels. If his wrongdoing makes him powerful and prosperous, so that his fellowmen "look up" to him, his conscience is all but to his existence. He does not know himself without his body. He silenced and he lives a happy life. He is respected and honored.

He is loved for his good deeds and forgiven easily the evil he may do, especially by those who benefit from it. He is surrounded by family and friends who admire him as "a man of parts." He is a fortunate man. Guilt? What guilt? So long as one has goods and does good, one need not worry about right and wrong. In fact the question of integrity is confusing and superfluous. Seek goods and avoid evils, and you shall be a happy man. You are right if you prosper, wrong if you fail. Prosper therefore, and the rightness of it will take care of itself. However, in the meantime, be careful not to make strong enemies. That is dangerous. You never know how and when they will get the upper hand, and you will lose everything. Hence, do not be too indifferent to what people call right and wrong, but remember also that there is nothing so right as success. Let success, therefore, be the first rule of your life.

We need not go on with the sermon. Whether men do or do not agree with us in theory, they are one with us in practice. The man who would fail rather than lie a little here and wrong a little there, is in hiding. When a man is safe in wrongdoing for the sake of some obvious good, his conscience is more than reasonable about the matter and will not make a record of it except in extremely serious cases, that is, cases where exposure would ruin him. Hence, there may be much truth in the observations of parsons and publicans alike that the sense of guilt is all but atrophied among us. Certainly, where there is minimum fear of human retaliation, the sense of wrong is reduced to a faint murmur, so that one can hardly tell just what is being said. True, there is some grumbling there, but it makes no sense. There is nothing to do but ignore it, and that is what is done by any man of sense.

Without the sense of guilt, men experience a new freedom and a new happiness. It is as though a heavy burden had been lifted from their shoulders. They appear to become light hearted and "happy go lucky." Their life becomes much more simple. The goods and evils before them become obvious and clear-cut. They know what they want, and what they do not want. They enjoy the goods they have, and reach out for more. All the while, their conscience is at ease so long as they keep out of jail. If in addition, their fellowmen speak well of them, the moral impulse within them is satisfied and they live in peace, with themselves as well as their fellowmen.

But alas, this idyllic vision is not quite real. There are indications that all is not well; that not to feel guilty is neither not to *be* guilty, nor to escape the effects of guilt. Men are no longer responsible before God. The "fear of God" is all but gone. But neither fear nor guilt has vanished from the human scene.

There is no proportion between our denial of guilt and our freedom from anxiety. On the contrary, the more certain we are of our innocence and the more unaware of our existence as persons, the more subject we are to anxiety. The human soul has become a soil fertile for growths at once bitter and poisonous. It is as though some evil spirit went about in it, unseen and unheeded, and threw out handfuls of some vile chemical which turned everything sour. Men without guilt and without despair have become anxious in all things, living with fears which are at once inexplicable and inevitable. Their denial of guilt and despair being absolute, so is their anxiety and the fears that flow from it. Our denial of guilt has turned us into a race of spiritual neurotics.

Men who feel innocent in general, are nevertheless plagued with both anxiety and guilt. They are not anxious about their lives, but they are anxious about everything in it. They are innocent in general, but guilt works in them in all their works. They do not worry about death, but they worry to death about their goods. They do not acknowledge guilt, but they are ready to accuse everyone else of being guilty; which indicates that they are not as innocent as they pretend to be. Men who are free to achieve anything they will, are nevertheless in bondage to powers which make the good life impossible.

There is a rational anxiety and one that is irrational. Where there is memory of evils suffered in the past and knowledge of the causes of these evils as present in one's vicinity, there is legitimate fear and apprehension. But the wholesale, diffuse, disproportionate, paralyzing anxiety which turns against everyone with unreasoning ill will, is an irrational anxiety which grows out of a hidden despair and an unmanageable inclination to see the stamp of radical evil in every vicissitude of our existence.

The same is true of guilt. Every man has done wrong. He has despaired of his life and turned against God. He has turned against his neighbor and treated him without love and justice. It is rational and natural for a man, therefore, to acknowledge his guilt and to seek deliverance from it. But a diffuse self-pity coupled with an uncritical sense of innocence, "guilty feelings" which ruin life without rhyme or reason, permanent restiveness together with boundless complacency and repeated upsurges of despair—these things bespeak a poison which has its source in an underground and hopeless guilt.

3. *ANSWERS TO OBJECTIONS*

According to the scientific and otherwise enlightened mind of our time, guilt is a social invention and the sense of guilt a left-over from the ages of superstition. Moreover, the havoc wrought by "guilt complex" in the lives of innumerable people has convinced the experts in mental hygiene that the very conception of guilt is a dreadful mistake and should be done away with as quickly as possible. It is expected that when this pestiferous notion of guilt is eliminated from our social life, there will dawn a new age of reason in which men will enjoy a new peace and welfare.

The truth is apparently on the side of such contentions. There is hardly a right which is not somewhere held to be wrong and hardly a wrong that is not deemed right by some people and done with no sense of guilt. Even deceit, adultery, murder, have been perpetrated with a clear conscience, while eating beef has been condemned as damnable. The changes in the rules of behavior in our own society make the doctrine of "the relativity of morals" both obvious and unquestionable. Hence, it is tempting to conclude that right and wrong represent the mores of a community of human beings.

The evil effects of guilty feeling are similarly obvious. A person convinced of having incurred guilt through an act of disloyalty or injustice, especially toward one who has a right to his friendship, suffers an inner devastation which has far reaching evil consequences in his life. Such a one is alienated from his fellowmen. He becomes anxious and apprehensive. He suspects others of indifference and even of malice. He is frustrated in his need for love and becomes generally hostile. He seeks to overcome his social disadvantages by acquiring power which shall give him security in spite of the ill will of those around him. He becomes wilful, arbitrary, unreasonable, and then, if possible, tyrannical. A man suffering from a "guilt complex" is also a man of lust and fills his life and the lives of his neighbors with enmity and conflict. So, the sense of guilt is an evil thing, and the more it is removed the better it is for any given community of people.

Nevertheless, in spite of all the enlightenment as to the origins and effects of the sense of guilt, in spite also of common repudiation of guilt, there has been no palpable diminution in anxieties and hostilities which are unintelligible except as consequences of guilt. Religion, the perennial source of the sense of guilt, is now, in this respect, quite harmless. Millions are convinced that "there is no right or wrong but thinking makes it so." Men violate most of the traditional taboos without any serious discomfort of conscience. But still, human relations are saturated with an anxiety which can only be due to common judgments of guilt. Our cautions with our fellowmen, our unwillingness to place ourselves under their power, our suspicions of foul play, our impulse to fortify ourselves against possible perfidy, our frequent wilfulness and will to test our power, our restlessness within ourselves—all these, with their infinite variations in mood and feeling, squeeze the joy out of our lives and remain inescapable witnesses to a guilt which cannot be removed either by theory or in practice.

In different communities men judge different acts as guilty. But in every community, in the civilized world at least, some acts are judged right and others wrong. When it comes to thieving, oppression, adultery, murder, and the like, there is almost universal agreement that they are wrong. Among us, it is considered wrong to lie, to deprive a man of his goods and honor, to treat him as one without reason or responsibility, to ignore his needs and sensibilities, etc. It is always necessary to be understanding and charitable. But one cannot treat all men as irresponsible, and one certainly cannot treat oneself as such. We are responsible to give each man his due as a human being. When we fail to be just, we are *eo ipso* guilty.

In our knowledge of things, we distinguish between truth and error. In our use of things, we distinguish between good and evil. In our relations to persons, we have to do with right and wrong. It is quite as stupefying to deny guilt in human relations, as it is to deny error in our knowledge of things, or to deny evil in our natural environment. The fact that we may be mistaken as to facts, or as to the effects of facts upon us, by no means obliterates the distinctions between truth and error, or between good and evil. So also, the differences of judgment as to right or wrong make it by no means superfluous to concern ourselves with the fact of guilt. Some men have indeed denied truth and error; others have denied good and evil. So, many have denied right and wrong. But it has been, and shall be, impossible to exist intelligently without making these distinctions. Where there are persons, there is guilt. In our relations with our fellowmen we can and do act as though they were not human beings; and as we do so act, we incur guilt. It is quite as foolish to ask why inhumanity should be guilty, as to ask why it should be erroneous to think the sea is full of ink or that sunshine is bad for one's garden.

Guilt is not a social invention, and its incidence is not limited to criminals and neurotics. It is true that guilt goes with fear. A fear-ridden society is also a guilt-ridden society. What follows? Is the sense of guilt, therefore, a social invention intended to make us behave ourselves? But, fear is usually quite sufficient for this end. The end of social cooperation for a common enjoyment of goods is served quite well when men learn to fear the consequences of opposing it. In point of fact, we behave well because we know "what is good for us." Why then the sense of guilt? What purpose does it serve? Why did men ever accuse themselves and others, rather others and themselves, of guilt? Was it not enough that they should have persuaded and frightened one another?

Even if we suppose that the sense of guilt, over against or beyond the sense of fear, is necessary for social cohesion, it does not follow that it could have been invented for the purpose. Reason and fear are essential for community life, but men do not deduce therefrom that thinking and fearing are social inventions. I think thus and so, I fear this and that, mainly and habitually, because I live in this particular society. But that I think at all and fear at all are due to capacities which I brought into the group in which I exist. Thinking and fearing are integral to my existence as a human being, and that is why I can be taught to think what I think and to fear what I fear. It would be extremely confusing if, because I think this and fear that, it were deduced that thinking and fearing are conventions in particular societies, and that some think and fear while others are free from such activities. It would not be obviously wise to say, "Many men think and fear to their great detriment. Many who do not think and fear live simple and free and happy lives. Therefore, let us cure all men of these bad habits of thinking and fearing." Besides, such an undertaking may be impossible because men might think and fear in spite of soundest medical advice and in spite of the evils which ensue from understanding and imagination. Similarly, if the sense of guilt is intrinsic to human personality, it is a hindrance to declare ourselves against it and to push it aside.

The opinion that the sense of guilt is due to social tradition alone is suggested by the fact that men feel guilty when they break a law or act contrary to custom. Since laws and customs are maintained by the authority of a given group, some think that the sense of guilt is merely a social product. Thus, it becomes habitual to think of guilt only in connection with law and custom. It is now assumed that a man feels guilty simply because he has broken a law and is afraid of the consequences of his actions.

But, guilt is not merely a matter of being at odds with law and custom. It is *social* law, *social* custom, which inspire the sense of guilt. A man does not feel guilty when he breaks a "natural law," especially when he does it in his ignorance. When a man ignores height and depth, or cold and heat, he may do himself great harm. He may regret his folly and promise himself to be less stupid in the future. But he does not feel guilty. It is the persons behind civil law and custom who evoke in us the sense of guilt. Laws and customs as such arouse us to fear. Lawbreaking is a fearful thing; the more serious its anticipated consequences, the greater the fear. But it is not, as such, guilty. The guilt in lawbreaking comes from the tacit acknowledgment that to act against law and custom is also to act against people. Guilt is the violation of persons, whether divine or human. It is rooted in personal existence, in existence in relation to persons, and cannot be rooted out without a repudiation of humanity. No sooner than I recognize another as a person, I also acknowledge the reality of guilt. Perchance I am not guilty in relation to this person. But, it never is true that I am not guilty in relation to all persons. It is never true that I am not guilty.

The essence of guilt is in some wrongness in our existence as persons. We are wronged as persons, and we wrong others who are persons. When we judge others guilty, it is not merely that we have suffered this or that evil. When we are maligned, when our goods are stolen, when we are ousted, or excluded, or tyrannized over, we are not merely deprived of this or that specific good. We are violated as persons. The wrongdoer is not acting toward us as persons, that is, he is indifferent to our destiny, which is in fact central to our existence as persons. In wronging us, he does not care whether we are alive or dead, as we ourselves most certainly do care. Therefore, our impulse is to take any act perpetrated against us as though it were a stab at the heart. Injuries are construed as signs of an ultimate denial of our existence as persons and therefore as tokens of an absolute enmity. When we judge a man guilty, we accuse him of inhumanity.

We cannot escape a similar judgment against ourselves when we wrong others. The terror of guilt is in the fact that we believe ourselves judged as we judge others. This man whom I have wronged recognizes me as an enemy, as one whose behavior towards him is based upon a denial of his existence as a person. He knows that I care nothing for his dread; that for me his death is a matter of radical indifference; that I am ready to gain an advantage over him, even though in doing so I may annihilate him. He assumes, as I assume, that the right way for men to act one toward another is to acknowledge their common dread as persons. It is to him a matter of truth and right that he be dealt with as one who lives in the shadow cast by nonbeing. When he is treated as one to whom nonbeing is irrelevant, as though he existed only in relation to goods, he is insulted and injured in the depths. When I wrong him, he takes it as a denial that any significance is to be attached to his existence as a unique history. He has read a warrant of his death, an unwarranted warrant, based upon a calumnious lie and issued in guilty indifference.

I know that this judgment of the man I have wronged is true. I know that the accusation of guilt against me is just. In relation to that man I exist in a lie. Hence, I am driven, by the contradiction in the wrong I have done, to regard and denounce myself as guilty. I have not simply judged something erroneously; I have treated someone wrongly. I have not simply been ignorant of something; I have ignored somebody. I have not simply misused something; I have violated a man. I have not simply done evil; I have done wrong.

The guilty man is guilty in relation to himself as well as to another. A man cannot wrong another without wronging himself. He cannot ignore another as a person without doing the same to himself. When he, for the sake of some advantage, causes another man to lose some good or goods, he denies his own dread as a person. He relates himself to being without at the same time acknowledging his existence as a person, that is, in relation to nonbeing. When he wrongs another for the sake of some gain, he wrongs himself by identifying the gain anticipated with the Good. He acts as though the thing gained filled the vacuum confronting him as a person. He lies to himself concerning himself even while he lies to the other concerning the other. And when a man lies to himself about himself, going so far as to deny to himself that he is a person, and doing it effectively by acting as though he were not a person, he is abysmally silly, and guilty. Thus, the guilty man is in a state of living self-contradiction.

4. *THE MYSTERY OF GUILT*

When a man lives as though he were not going to die, he repudiates his being in nonbeing and with it his relation to nonbeing. He construes his problem as one of survival rather than as one of existence. Thus the problem of his destiny in common with his fellowmen is set aside, and he is left with the problem of surviving them. Thus also, he sets himself in opposition to them both in being and in having. Involved in his competition for goods is the impulse for survival without which he can neither have nor enjoy. In fact, his having and enjoying assume a peculiar goodness as substantiating his survival. Thus he habituates himself to ignore his being in nonbeing and in relation to nonbeing, and to ignore the same in his relations to his fellowmen. Such ignoring is a peculiar species of lying to which guilt is attached as thirst is to a dry body.

The impulse for survival in man is guilty. In the animals,

this impulse is presumably natural. Coupled with the sexual urge, it is a means of continued existence for the species. The animal lives and breeds, and life goes on. When in the process, he kills other animals, as happens universally, there is no guilt involved. The animal is related only to the species. It exists and acts in that relation, and thereby exists and acts naturally.

But man is different. He does not exist only in relation to the species. Men seek power and possession beyond the necessities of survival for breeding. The human "struggle for existence" is obviously subject to an unlimited complication which is absent among the animals. It is shot through with fears, anxieties, bitterness, resentments, vengefulness, malice, pleasure in another's hurt, which go far beyond the conditions of racial survival. The struggle for existence among us is corrupted by despair. Hence, this natural struggle among the living, among us, becomes corrupt, lustful and guilty. Nobody is really deceived by the pretense that lust is natural. Therefore, men continue to feel guilty and to pass judgments of guilt, all theories to the contrary notwithstanding. So long as man acts contrary to nature, in himself and among men, he remains guilty and his guilt conditions his total behavior.

The human struggle for personal survival is based on the lie that to survive is to live "forever." This lie turns the impulse for survival into a lust for domination which is guilty. So long as this perversion occurs, guilt is inevitable. The lie of evading the despair in nonbeing permeates the totality of human existence, and men live in it, rather they die in it, hardly aware of the truth of their situation unless awakened to it occasionally by surprising incidences of evil which speak quietly but firmly of a radical wrong in the human soul. The transcendent despair of man with nonbeing drives him to turn his life into a lie, and this lie is at the roots of guilt.

Despair with life is a source of shame. Men are constantly driven either to disclaim their despair, or to justify it as "natural," or to divert themselves. But, in any case, they must live in it. Even when they consider despair foolish, or when they revel in its melancholy effects, they cannot do away with the undertone of guilt in it. A man who becomes sentimental about his despair is at once guilty and disgusting. But also, one who acts tough or indifferent is convicted of bad taste which also is guilty. The judgment of guilt is inseparable from this despair, whether it be in oneself or in others.

If man exists in relation to men and things alone, neither his indifference nor his despair is guilty. He loves things innocently in so far as they are lovable, and he despairs before death as a simple negation of his existence. He might be a worldling pursuing his pleasure, or a pessimist lost in his melancholy; and nobody would blame him whether he were the one or the other. But, one does not have to be greatly discerning to notice that immersion in the world of things and submersion in melancholy, both, are at once disgusting and guilty. No, a man ought not so to immerse and submerge himself. He ought to keep his head out of the water, lest he cease to breathe and die. Guilt implies that a man ought not to despair, even though he has no apparent reason not to despair. It suggests a self-imposed blindness to light, a radical estrangement from his true situation. It is as though his fate were a tragedy: as though he himself were responsible for the death working in his life. His misery is not the misery of one who has met an accident. It is the misery of one who is at once lost and guilty. He sits in the dark and waits for the end. But he might not have been in the dark. There is a light shut from his eyes, and the pity is that he cannot see in it. Still, the darkness itself is a dark light, and its gloom is suffused with a glory as that of the life which evokes the despair in him.

The strange truth is that man is guilty when he despairs in relation to nonbeing. This is on the face of it absurd because there is guilt only among persons. But "the face of it" is false. Man is guilty because the nonbeing he despairs of hides a Being whom alas he knows only in his ignorance of despair and guilt.

Guilt is darkness. It is the guilt in man that makes him to despair of his fellowmen and leads him to a life of lust. His lust energizes his guilt and makes him an enemy of his neighbor.

Guilt, as well known in the "age of faith" and rediscovered by mind healers in our time, is a very bad thing. It is even worse when repudiated and relegated to the subconscious which it poisons and turns into a seat of death. But still, the darkness of guilt contains a mystery which is the mystery of guilt itself. The strange thing is that despair is guilty and that the guilt in despair is a primary ingredient of lust. We know guilt only in relation to persons. And yet, we are guilty when we despair of the void. Despair of the void cannot be guilty because the void neither is a person, nor does it relate us to a person. But, despair *is* guilty—here is a contradiction which can be resolved by either denying guilt or by faith that the darkness we anticipate through death is other than the void we see in our despair. We are subject to the darkness of guilt because the original setting of our existence is not darkness but light. Guilt is a negative awareness of God who declares our despair guilty. Despair is a personal act, an act of repudiation and self-alienation, a refusal to acknowledge that for us to exist is to live and move and have our being in God. Hence it is guilty. Guilt is shadow cast by the light of God. It is revealed to us by God as the foretaste of faith which marks our restoration to our natural existence as God's creatures whose light and good is God.

Guilt repudiated means death. Guilt acknowledged by us and removed by God, means life.

5. THE NEW INNOCENCE AND LUST FOR POWER

Guilt has a way of hiding itself behind despair. The man who disowns his relation to Being, and thereby sees nonbeing as nothingness, becomes a pessimist, and it is characteristic of pessimism that it excludes the sense of guilt. The pessimist is a nihilist. He knows and acknowledges the obvious fact that he has no future. There is an evil awaiting him which is like no other evil. There is an absolute darkness and an absolute emptiness awaiting him, beside which his life with all the evil in it is an absolute good. The nothingness before him is like no other nothingness. It is his end, the end of his world, and the end of all that happens in him and to him in the world. Here, man the thing confronts nothing, and despairs with a unique and ultimate despair. This despair overwhelms the sense of guilt, and man comes to regard himself as the victim of Necessity. He may be guilty in a dozen ways, in his relations to law and custom. But he is not guilty as he exists in relation to his destiny.

The repudiation of guilt is the product of despair and self-pity. Man is so profoundly and persistently aware of a wrong against his very being, that he will not take seriously the wrongs he does against others. What are all his wrongdoings compared with the desperate wrong under which he exists and must exist by necessity: the wrong of his own annihilation? One man has killed another. That is bad, and men say he is very gravely guilty. But what is that compared with the wrong of his own end in the void? After all, the murdered man was not immortal. A man has deprived others of their property, or liberty, or security. That is bad, and men say he is guilty. But what about the wrong whereby he himself shall be deprived of life itself? Certainly, there is no wrong he has done or can do which can compare with the wrong of his own fate. He is the wronged and not the wrongdoer. Hence, there is in him a Resentment which demolishes all resentment against him, an Innocence which banishes all guilt, a self-pity which is a perennial and adequate means of self-justification. The man is simply speaking "not guilty." The firm and often fierce denial of guilt by the modern man is inspired by a new despair concerning human destiny.

The new innocence is a delusion. It veils the sense of guilt, but it cannot remove guilt itself. Hence men go on judging their neighbors guilty and expecting to be judged likewise. There still is no telling where one is going to be wronged. One must be ready to suffer injustice in the hands of all but one's most reliable friends. One must not trust even these with all one's goods. One must never be completely at any one's disposal. One must have enough power to protect oneself against anyone and in any situation.

Guilt is a permanent factor in human relations. It marks a radical estrangement between man and man, and sets them in opposition one to another. Thus opposed, men have no choice but to seek to dominate one another and to increase their several powers for use one against another.

Guilt in relation to others includes, as we have shown, guilt in relation to ourselves. When we violate others, we also violate ourselves and exist in self-contradiction. The guilty man is confused and confounded within himself. He cannot follow either his own good or that of another. In this state, he tyrannizes over himself, making himself to act without regard to reason or to good. He lords it over himself and derives his deepest satisfaction from his own wilfulness. He becomes possessed of an "ego" which can exist only in domination over himself and his fellowmen alike. He is estranged both from himself and from others, and exists in a general opposition to all men including himself. Such opposition generates lust for power, and lust for power energizes the opposition. Both the opposition and the lust are guilty. But our "innocent" man cannot admit guilt. He disavows his guilt and gives himself up to a lying self-pity; and the man of self-pity is a singleminded man of lust. His lust is immune to self-criticism, and without self-criticism he is free to follow his lust; rather he is in bondage to it. His lust for power covers his guilt and acts as an antidote to his sense of guilt. But in this way, it can neither remove his guilt nor even mitigate it. On the contrary, the lust quickens the guilt and makes it an active source of conflict and misery, both within himself and among his fellowmen.

The guilty man must always justify himself because existence in self-contradiction is not tolerable; and he does. He lies to himself and to others, pretending to be innocent while he is guilty. As he lies, he loses his grip upon truth, and without truth he can exist only through power. In hiding his guilt, he learns to hate himself and arouses the resentment of others because of his hypocrisy. His self-hatred turns his love for the good into a lust for power, and the resentment of his fellowmen makes the same lust indispensable, both for protection against them and for self-justification among them. Hence it is that our age of pretended innocence is also an age of lust for power.

A guilty man must show that he is innocent, while others are guilty. He must show that he is good, whereas others are evil. But, nobody can bear to be guilty, or wrong, or evil. Hence a man who justifies himself turns others against himself and makes them his enemies. Thus the world is filled with enmity and enmity makes lust for power inevitable.

Guilt, unacknowledged, energizes the lust for power, and lust for power, also unacknowledged, adds to the virulence of guilt. Guilt leads to lust and lust to guilt. This is "the vicious circle" which grows smaller and smaller, and makes for the panic of life for which the only remedy is death; unless, of course, it be broken through a removal of guilt and a returning. of lust into love.

CHAPTER VI

Man in Isolation

A. THE NEW DESPAIR

1. THE SOUL OF THE WESTERN MAN

THE MODERN MAN is possessed of a new conviction that he lives in a void. The erstwhile ambiguity in the recoil from finitude has disappeared. The great question of "the meaning of life," that is, the question of man's lifetime in relation to his perduring world, has been answered in the negative. The world has a future. The race has a future. Civilization has a future. There is a future for institutions, cultures, customs, skills, technics, for all things impersonal and repeatable. This unrepeatable person alone is confronted with extinction; and there is a conviction abroad that there is no doubt about this matter.

The "Western man" cannot entertain this conviction without a potent and consequential resentment. For centuries, he has lived in the light of the Christian "revelation." For centuries, "the Christian epic," with its incredible anthropology, has formed the mind of the Western man and conditioned his total existence. It has become second nature for him to believe in "God the Father Almighty, the Maker of heaven and earth." He has believed that God created man in His own image and destined him for eternal life in His Presence; that this man sinned against God in disobedience and incurred the punishment of death; that in the fulness of time God the Father Almighty sent His own Son into the world in order to deliver man from sin and death, and thus to accomplish His original intention of a "blessed immortality" for him. The story goes on with the crucifixion of the Son of God for man's salvation, His resurrection from the dead, the coming of the Holy Spirit, the founding of the Church "outside of which there is no salvation," and the continued labors of the Lord which shall be until the end of the world when all men shall be judged by the Son of God and shall receive their reward in either life everlasting in heaven or "eternal death" in hell.

Such a view of "human nature and destiny" gave the Western man a unique conception of his position in his world. In fact, he was in the world but not of it. He was a pilgrim, a sojourner, in this world of beginnings and endings. His true home was in a Beyond which was eternal as well as free from sin. He, the individual, indivisible, living person existed in relation to the eternal God and would one day find his abiding place with Him. He was no mere "concretion of eternal objects" (to use the language of Alfred North Whitehead) soon to become unconcreted again for further and different concretions in the flux of nature. He was a person who would one day answer for his deeds, and he himself, and not someone else, would receive his deserts for the right and wrong he had done. It was he who had sinned, he who was to die, he for whom the Son of God had come into the world, he who was to meet his Maker, he who was to go to heaven or hell. When God dealt with him, it was with him that He dealt and not with his neighbor. It was he who would rejoice in heaven or gnash his teeth in hell, not someone else. In short, he was he, and not someone else. He never was someone else, nor ever would be. He was someone, and would forever be someone, whether in heaven or in hell.

One might deduce from all this that the "Christian Hope" did away with "the tragic sense of life." If a man is destined for eternal life, then death is a simple transition to another life and a matter of indifference. Doubtless such was the professed view of the Christians and many turned it into an occasion of superstition and complacency. But the greater effect of the Christian faith was *to reveal* the "tragedy of life." By teaching the ultimate and eternal status of personal existence, Christianity produced a sense of selfhood which became an active source of the sense of tragedy. The same faith which led men to exist as persons and to "hope in God," produced a new seriousness in the presence of sin and death. In fact, Christianity revealed the full meaning of the tragedy of human existence by insisting upon man's responsibility for sin and death at the same time that it recognized the inevitability of both.

By tying sin and death together, Christianity created a new dimension in human self-consciousness. Death established man's relation to nonbeing, but sin established his relation to God. The recoil from finitude was now bound with recoil from sin. Man assumed a new responsibility toward "truth, mercy, and peace" before God. He now despaired of righteousness as he also despaired of life. He existed both in relation to Being and in relation to nonbeing. The Christian faith qualified dread by inducing men to fear damnation rather than death. But the terror of the "second death" fixed attention upon the "first death," in terms of both sin and death, so that the recoil from finitude was energized rather than removed by faith in the resurrection of the dead. With apparent paradox, the Christian faith emphasized the "problem of existence" by its claim that it was solved. The greater the hope, the greater became the dread. The brighter the light from heaven, the darker became the light upon this earth. The more secure the destiny of man seemed, the more edifying discourse became somber and full of dread. The new sense of personal existence which went with the Christian hope quickened the dread in the human soul. Concern with sin confirmed the concern with death and induced a restlessness which could end only beyond death.

Christianity established a vital ambiguity in the soul of man. It made existence itself ambiguous. The Christian mind, especially when it was serious, had to live with a faith compounded of hope and despair. The Gospel of victory over sin and death revealed the true dimensions of the warfare which is the life of man upon the earth. A new hope and a new dread acted one upon the other with a new and boundless energy.

Together, they produced an ambiguity which is at the source of Western civilization and culture. The dynamics of this civilization, with its succession of "ages" and its continuous restlessness, with its zeal for knowledge and power, its political and economic revolutions, its endless philosophical inquiries and tireless artistic activity—the dynamics of this whole breathtaking historical existence called Western culture, can be neither discerned nor understood without reference to the creative ambiguity in the spirit of the Western man. This ambiguity whereby the Western man is oriented at once toward heaven and toward hell, toward life and toward death, toward substance and toward shadow, toward form and toward formlessness, toward peace and toward war, toward justice and toward tyranny, toward community and toward chaos, toward an all inclusive and eternal "Yea" and toward an all excluding and irrevocable "Nay"—this boundless and all-informing ambiguity is definitive of both the essence and existence of the Western man. Without it neither he nor his civilization nor his culture can exist. When he loses this ambiguity, he loses everything: his social freedoms, his philosophy and his art, yea, in the longer run, even his science and his machines. He loses his soul, and everything is in jeopardy: as it is today. He ceases to exist as a person. He despairs and, to say the least, aids in his own destruction.

The frightful thing in the Western world today is that apparently too many men have come to repudiate the ambiguity of human existence. Ambiguity is now replaced with contradiction. The Western man has the ego of a god with the destiny of a dog. He knows himself as an unrepeatable, irreplaceable person. He is at the same time convinced that he is a thing of time and space doomed to extinction. The dynamic equilibrium between faith and dread is now upset. The tragic sense of life, born of the paradoxical understanding of the greatness and the littleness, the freedom and the bondage, of man, is all but gone. The Western man is left with an ego which is inflated but empty. His is the misery of a dethroned king who can neither forget the past nor face the future. He is as a man turned out of his house and home, and left alone to roam upon roads which lead nowhere. He is lost in both space and time, coming from nowhere and going nowhere, begun with nothing and to end as nothing. The problem of life—the metaphysical problem—is now solved. It is solved in the negative. The answer is "nothing." Time has now become the vehicle of death, and death the gateway to the void.

2. *BEHIND THE NEW DESPAIR*

In spite of occasional hesitation or heresy among philosophers, the Christians, prior to the end of the eighteenth century, believed that they lived in a finite world. Pious Catholics and Protestants alike resisted the suggestion that the world might be infinite. They attributed infinity to God alone, and that in "being" rather than in extension. Their total world was spherical. It was a perfect world, and not endless. It was a world with spheres within spheres, and its utmost boundaries contained heaven above and hell below. The earth was at the center of the world and the marvelous bodies in the heavens rotated around it. This world was by no means small. It was immense enough to give men some sense of the greatness and glory of the Creator. Nonetheless, it was finite. The Christian existed in a number of relations which made up the totality of his world. He was completely oriented. He came from nowhere; it is true; for God created him. But, now that he was upon the earth, he was going somewhere. He might go to heaven, either directly or by way of purgatory. He might, alas, go to hell and suffer eternal torment. But, in any case, he was going somewhere. Being on his way somewhere, he was doubtless, now, somewhere. He had had a beginning. Now he was upon the earth. In the future, he would be forever in heaven or in hell. Thus, he existed in relation, both in space and in time.

Man is an extended being, and his extension is essential to his existence. He does not know himself without his body. He is a body. He is a body among bodies and is oriented to his world as a body. He knows where he is in relation to the other bodies around him. He lives at 26 Belair Road. His shop is at 64 State Street. The restaurant where he eats is at 138 High Street. The movie house, the barber shop, the school, the church, the hospital, the police station, the library, etc., are located at definite points in his environment. Together, they constitute a finite world in which he knows where he is and in which he is at home. He goes to one place, and comes back from another, and is at home. Everything is at a given distance. Everything exists in a set of finite relationships. Hence, he is not lost. Of course, beyond his own little world, there is one which he does not know so well. The town where he lives is in a county; the county is in a state, the state in a country, the country on a continent, the continent upon the earth. The earth is among the stars, and beyond the stars there are more stars. Still, his world is limited, and he is at home.

Such at homeness is both external and internal. He is at home both in body and in mind. He is at home in mind because he is at home as a body. His mind imagines his world and reflects upon his relationships with his world. It is preoccupied with things animate and inanimate, and with their relations to himself. Thus the mind mirrors the position of the body and shares the at homeness of the body in its finite world. It is full as the world is full. It is meaningful as the world is meaningful. It is essentially at peace in the world because its beloved and indispensable body is oriented and at home.

Take a man away from his "home town," put him in a hotel in a strange city, and he is lost. He may soon locate a few places and learn his way around in his vicinity. He may even make some friends. But still, he is a stranger. He is surrounded by unknown places, unknown streets leading heaven knows where. He is oriented to some places, but he is a stranger. His environment extends indefinitely into a void, and creates a void within him. In spite of being related to some things, he is unrelated. In spite of knowing a few objects, he is ignorant of his setting and lost in it. He is self-conscious and cautious, wondering if he understands what is going on around him and ready for a surprise or two. With his body disoriented, he is anxious; and in spite of the good he may meet, he is ready for some evil which shall be his undoing. In short, he is lost in body and bewildered in mind.

Such is the position of the modern man in the Newtonian world of "infinite space." The man in a strange city hopes that one day he will find himself in a finite place and find his true position in it. In the modern world, there is no such expectation. Ours is a world in which the imagination cannot come to a decent rest. It is not only immense beyond imagining, which is horrible enough, but also a world without boundaries, without a top, or bottom, or sides to it. The furthermost stars, unimaginably distant from us, are still on this side of the limits of the universe. Their positions are upon lines which have no ending, and their locations have no intelligible relation to the whole of being. In fact, there is no whole of being. We no longer live in a universe. Space has become a matter of unlimited extension, and everything in it is lost. The substitution of an "infinity of worlds" for the "perfect world" of the ages of faith means a radical dislocation of everything. There is no "simple location." The earth is not at the center of the world; heaven is not at the circumference of it; and this for the reason that the world has neither center nor circumference. Every body related to another body is also related to no body; that is, it is unrelated; that is, it is lost. In a world which is boundless, every line is an endless line, and every body is a lost body. No matter how well charted a portion of our world is, once we are aware of infinite extension, we are confronted with a vacuum which makes everything insubstantial. All relations in a setting of unrelation become unreal. All meanings in an unrelated world become meaningless. Existence becomes radically unintelligible, and there is a persistent suspicion that it is a delusion.

Of course, such a view of the things in an endless world

is not reasonable. Whether the world be finite or not finite, things are what they are and they exist in the relations in which they do in fact exist. What do the thingness of the thing and the goodness of the good have to do with whether the world has or does not have an end? Why cannot one cultivate his backyard without troubling his head about its ultimate setting? The backyard is the backyard even if it were set in an endless world containing only a limited number of backyards. Meaning and extension are incommensurate one to the other. Hence, it is irrational to deny relation in an unrelated world, and it is foolish to despair in it.

Nonetheless, the despair is there and we must account for it. It may be unreasonable, but it is not without reason. The despair of the mind in the modern world is too prevalent and too persistent to be the outcome of incidental perversity. It is rooted in our common awareness that we exist in an endless vacuum. No matter how hard we try, and we try very hard, we cannot talk ourselves out of our lostness in our world. We are spatial beings and we exist in spatial relations. The apparent, and to us very real, fact that these relations are unrelated make us subject to the persistent intuition that we are lost. We are at home and not at home. We are at home among things and lost in their setting. Being lost in the setting of our world, we are also lost in it. Hence, no matter how preoccupied we are with the things around us, we carry within us the conviction that we are in fact lost. Just as a man in a strange land may find a haven in a corner of it without ceasing to be lost, so we also come and go without knowing whence we come and where we go. With the body lost, the mind cannot but despair; for they together constitute the man.

3. *MAN WITHOUT NEIGHBORS*

The finite world of tradition was a *plenum*. Hosts of living beings, both good and evil, peopled the earth and all the spheres of the cosmos. Man was a neighbor to angels and demons who acted like all true neighbors in making his business their own.

The angels guided him toward good and the devils toward evil, but both angels and devils made him feel at home in his world. They peopled the various spheres within the firmament and went to and fro between heaven or hell and the earth. No matter how ghostly, elusive, unpredictable, and even troublesome, still they were alive and interested. Even the beasts became involved in this spiritual society, and entered the common life of men and angels. The spirits of the dead refused to be excluded from their former habitation, or at least from an interested view of the goings on in it. The saints looked down from heaven; the damned, up from hell; and those in the purgatory were a source of constant warning and encouragement to their friends upon the earth as well as beneficiaries of their kindness. The whole world was a scene of warlike activity, in which God and the Devil, the Former with His hierarchy of good spirits and the latter with his legions of evil spirits, contended for the souls of men and filled the spaces with the sound and fury of their zeal. Still, God the Father, God the Son, God the Holy Spirit, together with their angels, ascending and descending, lightened the whole world with their Presence and revealed it as an inn on the way to man's eternal home.

We, on the other hand, must live with the awareness that all the heavenly bodies except our earth may well be devoid of life; that man upon this planet is the only intellectual existence in the vast spaces of the universe; that we have no neighbors, neither friends nor enemies, anywhere in this indefinitely extended world. Man today is like one who suddenly wakes up to find himself in an oasis surrounded by an interminable desert. And he soon finds out that he is among utter strangers who do not and never will understand his language. It is inevitable that such a man should be lonely, that the emptiness around him should impress itself upon his mind, so that he should be empty within, as his world is empty without. It is needless to add that his total existence, his thoughts, feelings, actions, are conditioned by his situation.

It is interesting and not uninstructive to observe how men

living in the "Copernican world" have done their best to see the universe as a *plenum.* They have done their pathetic best to make themselves believe that this vast world is a huge organism teeming with lesser organisms. The more the world expanded under the gaze of man, the more hectic became the desire to fill it up with beings who would be kin and kind to man. From Giordano Bruno to Alfred North Whitehead, mystics, idealists, rationalists, romanticists, vitalists, spiritualists, alike, have tried to make out that man is not alone in his world. It seems as though every possible device in epistemological and cosmological speculation has been employed in order to show that there is a deep continuity between man and his environment. It has been argued that, if nothing else, since the world is intelligible, since man can and does know something somewhat, he is not altogether lost. Prudent men, philosophers and laymen alike, have turned their eyes studiously away from space and fixed them upon the objects around them, thus creating the illusion that the world is finite and quite manageable. Thus they have talked themselves into being at home although they confessed that they did not quite know what on earth was going on. Were it not for the void around them, they might all have become Aristotelean realists and declared "the ontological problem" virtually solved; which would have meant the achievement of a new at-homeness in the world. But the void is there. The universe is too large for neighborly relations and there is too much empty space for anybody's home.

a. *The Philosopher*

It is interesting to ask: Why is it that modern philosophy has been, in the main, an endless disputation on epistemology and cosmology, that is, on what-do-we-know and what-is-anything? Why have there been, in the modern world, endless and confounding arguments on mind and body, freedom and determinism, idealism and materialism, rationalism and empiricism, realism and pragmatism, vitalism and intuitionism versus mechanism and experimentalism, and the "scientific method"? Even a superficial glance at such concerns of philosophic thought since Descartes makes it evident that men have been extremely busy avoiding a vision of the world at large. Modern philosophy might well be named the Great Introversion or the Conspiracy against the Whole. Give the modern philosopher something, anything, and let him think it over. He has all he needs in order to keep him occupied indefinitely. Does he see what he sees? Is what he sees the thing he sees? Does he see an image of the thing? Does he see more than the image of the thing? What is the relationship between the image and the thing, between the image and his eyes, between his eyes and his mind? Is there a thing? Does he have a mind? Is the image "given" or is it "a construct"? If it is both, how much of each is it? Is the idea of the thing the same as the image? If the idea is not the same as the image, provided there is an image, where do ideas originate, and what do they really reveal about the object? Maybe there is nothing but the subject which we do not experience; and the subject may be nothing at all but a locus of images which are themselves nothing in particular.

It may well be that with Descartes there began a race of thinkers who attained a new subtlety and critical acumen. It may be that Plato, Aristotle, St. Thomas, were too naïve to appreciate fully the problems involved in being and knowing. Still, it may also be that the skeptical and agnostic orientations of modern philosophy are instinctive reactions to the modern man's lostness in his world. A man who is lost is a natural skeptic. He is not inclined to believe everything he sees or hears. Everywhere he turns, he wonders if he is not being made a fool of. He goes about cautiously, questioning and holding back. He doubts everything, and begins to doubt even himself. He asks the same questions over and over again, without arriving at a satisfactory answer. He seeks peace by cultivating a few stable relations, by saying to himself, "This at least I have and this in any case I know." But he remains restless. He tries to lose himself in his little backyard and to forego asking where he is and where he may be going. He even talks himself into believing that such questions are silly. If a neighbor asks them of him, he becomes an Olympian and pushes him aside saying: "Sir, I am a philosopher and not a fool. The questions you ask are unworthy of a mind such as mine. They are nonsensical. Now, I will teach you to ask some real questions. How do you know that you are talking to me and that you hear what I say? How do you know that you are sitting on that chair and that you can get up whenever you want to? How do you know that there is a you who is sitting on something you call a chair and asking that silly question about the meaning of life? Sir, these are real questions. And I am very busy thinking about them. So you will be so kind as to leave me alone. Good day to you. But consider, what is good? What is day? What are you? And what does that little "to" mean? Semantics, sir, semantics, is what you really need. Good day to you."

The *faux pas* in modern philosophy was not so much "the dualism" of Descartes, as a largely unconscious but determined and persistent conspiracy to turn aside from man's plight in the modern world. The best clue for the understanding of modern philosophy is the fact that the modern man is lost. It is the lost man in the philosopher who has persuaded him to question the existence of the person. There has been a strange agreement among modern philosophers that the "I" does not exist. Empiricists, idealists, rationalists, materialists, pragmatists, have agreed upon this point. Nothing that cannot be thought can be known to exist. The "I" who is supposed to do one's thinking cannot itself be thought. Therefore, the "I" cannot be known to exist. Again: in so far as anything is known to exist, it is known to exist as an object and in relation to other objects. The subject is not known to exist as an object and in relation to objects. Therefore, the subject cannot be known to exist. Hence, the "I" cannot be thought as lost in its world. The dread and despair of man with regard to his destiny are due to misconceptions. No real philosopher should take them seriously.

On the one hand, the despair of man in the Newtonian world finds widespread expression in the doctrine of the non-existence of the person. On the other hand, it has given rise to the equally radical doctrine of the non-existence of the world. We cannot let the infinite swallow us; so, we would swallow the infinite! After all, every object that is known is also an idea. No object is known except as idea, and nothing is idea except as thought. Nothing is thought except to a mind, and I know no mind but my own to which the world is an idea. The mind, therefore, which thinks is alone really real, and the world it thinks is merely its own idea. The whole of this apparently infinite world is posited by the *ego* and has no reality apart from it. It is not man that is in the world but the world that is in man. Man is the lord of time and space, especially of space. He does not exist in space. He only thinks spatially. Extension is not outside but inside of him. Infinite extension signifies only his own boundless and timeless ego. In short, he is not lost in his world. His dread and despair are due to his lack of philosophic acumen. No real philosopher should take them seriously . . .

So, my dear wanderer, you can make your choice. Either you do not exist, or your world does not exist. In either case, you are not lost. Of course, being either non-existent in your world, or not having a world in which you might exist, you cannot be at home. But, then, you are not lost. Is that not enough? Must you also be at home? In fact, you should forget the whole thing. Epistemology, cosmology, metaphysics, ontology, axiology, esthetic theory, sociology, psychology, logic, mathematics, science and semantics, all these and more will keep you busy all the days of your life. Think on these things, my dear fellow, and you will have neither the time nor the zeal to worry your head about your destiny. We'll tell you a secret. You have no future in this world, and there is no other world in which you might have it. But it is futile to discuss this subject. You should not do it. Your fellow philosophers do not like it. Remember, you may discuss everything else, and there is a great deal of everything. You may even turn a reformer. But keep away from "the problem of destiny."

If there is any subject that has worried the modern philosopher it is whether he knows anything as it really is. He suffers from a chronic skepticism, and that in spite of all the triumphs of science and technology under his very nose. Now we have knowledge which is power and has every appearance of being knowledge of the real thing. At the same time, there has never been such widespread skepticism in the Western world. Soon after Newton had filled the world with the light of scientific truth, Kant had to come along and argue, meticulously and overwhelmingly, that we do not know the real thing as it really is. Since then, the skeptical mind of Kant has become public property, wandering between dogmatism and agnosticism, but never coming to a rest. Whence this skepticism? Why does the mind keep wandering? Why are we lost in our minds even while we know our way around in our world better than any generation before us?

Modern skepticism is the lostness of the mind of a lost body. There are times when the body acts as though it had no mind, and times when the mind acts as though its body did not matter. But by nature the mind thinks the fortunes of the body and follows its career with an absolute seriousness. When the body is in trouble, or lost, so is the mind. The mind of a man whose body is lost, is a skeptical mind. And there is nothing that will dispel his skepticism while his body is lost. The mind of a body which is dislocated and disoriented cannot solve the epistemological problem no matter how subtle and refined it becomes. Such a mind ends in frustration and becomes "pragmatic," that is, it lives from hand to mouth. In this way, skepticism is not overcome. It is pushed aside. Just as the lost man turns purely practical and immerses himself in the objects of his immediate environment, so his mind turns pragmatic and identifies knowledge with skill and power. Pragmatism is the last refuge of a skeptical mind. For three centuries, lost men have tried to convince themselves that they are not lost; or, that they know what they know. They have failed. Pragmatism is the lost man's attempt to save face. The face may be saved, but the man is still lost.

b. *The Romantic Poet*

The philosopher is a man preoccupied with thinking. Hence his lostness finds expression in a perennial indecision of the mind with regard to knowledge. But man is more than a thinker .He responds to his situation with his sensibilities as well as with his sense. When he becomes preoccupied with his feelings, he may lose something in the refinement and subtlety of his thought. But what he loses is made up for in a more direct and illuminating awareness of his situation. Such a man, the artist, whatever his medium, opens our eyes to the living truth of our existence as persons and discloses the sources of our thoughts as well as feelings in our response to the world in which we live. Hence poetic vision is indispensable for a proper insight into the human situation.

The predominant poetry of the modern world has been the Romantic, and the prevailing intention of such poetry has been to find the infinite in the finite. Flowers, birds, beasts, children, ruined remnants from the past, sunsets, seas, life, love, death, anything and everything, are fixed upon with a terrific expectancy and passion, with the hope that something will give us the clue to everything. The romantic poet is moved with the immovable intuition that if the meaning of the whole is to be discerned at all, it must be discerned in the part. For the nineteenth century poet, the knowledge of anything, an adequate awareness of anything in its external relations had become hopeless. The classical conviction that the part is known fully and richly only by its position in a pattern of external relations had now become foolish. Hence, the poet tried to apprehend the real not extensively but intensively. He hoped that by staring at one thing, no matter what thing, long enough, passionately enough, absorbedly enough, he would be able to say, "Ha! Now I know the really real. Now I have penetrated to the heart of truth. By knowing this one thing as I now know it, I know all that I need to know. I do not need to know anything else. I do not need to know too many things. I certainly do not need to know everything. Now that I have exposed the innermost essence of this one thing, I know the one thing that matters and with it I know the truth of all possible things."

Such intuitive knowledge, such apprehension of the bottom of being, is a very peculiar kind of knowledge. Communicable knowledge, knowledge that can be shared, knowledge which makes for society and a common culture, is extensive knowledge, knowledge which reveals order and connection. Anything absolutely simple and unrelated cannot be known. Yet, it is precisely such a thing that the romantic mind sought to comprehend. Not only that, it sought to convince itself that by knowing such a thing, it knew all that was worth knowing. And the reason for this quixotic quest was that the romantic man despaired of knowing anything in its setting of the whole. The whole he saw, rather did not see and despaired of seeing, was endless and the endless cannot be seen as a whole. The romantic poet, the modern poet, was lost in the new endless world. Hence, he despaired of a synthetic and unifying vision. He hoped that by feeling a single object strongly enough, he might achieve an awareness which would enable him to comprehend the core of the really real Reality. What he achieved was, in fact, a powerful self-stimulation. As everybody knew, he fancied things. He even went mad. People ceased to take him seriously, and that made him resentful and madder still.

The lost man is all feeling, and little mind. Hence, the lost man as a poet disavowed all intention of understanding. He turned the world of facts over to the scientist and cultivated his moods and fancies. He felt and expressed buoyancy, gloom, bitterness, peace, nostalgia, hope, etc. But, no one was sure, least of all himself, as to what the uproar was about. He felt a great deal, but he understood next to nothing. He projected himself and his emotions to everything around him. He moved about in a daze, and "saw things." "Nature" assumed a curious animation and induced a million moods. Men reverted to the animism of the proverbial savage mind, except that it now was without innocence and moderation. Thus the lonely man of the modern world went about winking at things without eyes or soul, and fancied himself surrounded with kin and friends. Romantic fancy, with its deep dislike for reason, was a desperate effort at being at home in a world where man is alone and lost.

No amount of false feeling and false prosody was enough to dissipate the *horror vacui* in the soul of the poet. It was as though everything bright and gay concealed a deep and dark terror. The romantic man was fascinated with ruins in moonlight, with deserts and deep forests, with rotting leaves and death of every sort. He sang cheerfully, it is true. But he was at his best when in "pursuit of death," when he could clothe things with pathos and lose himself in melancholy emotion. Here he achieved an overwhelming cadence and became abysmally sad. His happiness was usually strained and not too convincing. But when he turned somber and groaned in the depths, he was very effective; even though one did not know what all the sorrow and sadness was about.

The romantic poet was apparently sentimental, and so were many who wept with him. There was a palpable disproportion between the mood and its various occasions. It is almost impossible to read, for instance, Byron, Shelley, Carlyle, or Victor Hugo, without embarrassment. It is very disconcerting to think while one reads romantic literature. Nevertheless, contempt for the romanticists is in bad taste and a sign of deep stupidity. Even though the romantic poet or composer did not know what was ailing him, he had the humanity and sensibility to feel the despair of man in the modern world. He was indeed egotistical, fanciful, non-rational. But, in truth, he was not sentimental. The things around him, more or less trivial, were occasions for a renewed awareness of his plight in the modern world. His immoderate self-consciousness, his recurrent moods of gloom and despair, his self-delusion about his world, his preoccupation with his feelings in the abstract, his pretensions to some esoteric awareness, his verbal music intended only to create a mood, his lying use of rhythm and meter when his mind was at a standstill—all this, and more also, must not blind us to the fact that the romantic movement was a many-sided and eloquent expression of the despair of man in the world of Newton. Given the endless and all but empty world of the modern man, "Critical philosophy" and the "Romantic Movement" alike were inevitable. All honor to the skeptical philosopher for keeping his head; but honor also to the Romantic artist for keeping his heart.

c. *The Layman*

The Catholic Christian faith, as found in the Apostles' Creed, has become incredible to the common man as well as to the philosopher and poet. Today men doubt or deny it as readily as their forebears believed it. What was, in spite of all the mystery in it, reasonable, has now become unreasonable. What was rational or suprarational, has now become contradictory to reason. There are modernized versions of the faith, and very good arguments in support of them. The older versions themselves have their competent champions and good minds which still believe them. Nevertheless, the common man has become a confirmed and practical agnostic. Even though he may go to church and profess to believe its doctrine, he is possessed of a strong and persistent suspicion that the whole thing may be untrue. Certainly, in his daily life, whether he be a shopkeeper or a statesman, he arranges his affairs as well as he can without the benefit of his professed religion. He acts as an unbeliever, which is to say, in fact, he is one.

What is behind the new atheism? What leads the modern man, as over against his forebears, to reject the Apostles' Creed with this new certainty of unbelief? Why is our man so certain that there is not a heaven and that there is not a hell, and that the dead shall not arise? The reasons usually given to such questions do not explain the intuitive and presumptive certainty of modern unbelief. These reasons themselves need explanation. The astronomers have not located heaven and hell. But, then, they have not scanned every nook and corner in the universe. Again, it is said that the modern man demands verified knowledge. Very well. The existence of heaven and hell has not been verified. But, their non-existence also has not been verified. Again, unbelief is said to be due to secular education, materialism, worldliness, and the like, which prejudice men against the Christian faith. But then, are secularism and materialism self-explanatory? Certainly, these are not fortuitous aberrations of the modern spirit. There is something else behind them. Finally, the explanation of unbelief by sin is worthless for understanding the new dimension of intuitive certainty in the modern aversion to the Christian faith. None of these usual reasons given for unbelief, neither others like them, nor the sum total of them, explain the spontaneous, unreasoned, established, unquestioning, effective, unbelief of the vulgar man in the modern world.

Now, God of the Christian faith is *alpha* and *omega*, the First and the Last. Heaven and hell also are the first and the last. God, heaven and hell, are the ultimate positions which gave position to man in his world. When heaven and hell cease to be the setting of man's bodily existence, that is, when the body ceases to have a finite setting, there arises a series of questions which are extremely embarrassing to the vulgar mind. Where, pray, is God? Where is heaven whence the Son of God came for the salvation of man? Where did Christ go when He rose from the dead? Where shall the risen dead of mankind go? And where shall they have "the life everlasting"? Since it is not possible to imagine a place beyond the endless spaces of our world, the image-ridden mind of the vulgar finds the existence of God, and with it the whole of the Christian faith, at once unthinkable and incredible. Thus to the mind of an unoriented body, atheism becomes a second instinct.

The scientific and philosophical objections to the Christian faith are, for the vulgar mind, rumors rather than reasons. They are accepted with minimum of argument because there is, in the modern mind, a new and peculiar bias toward atheism. This bias is prior to rational and practical grounds which are proposed in the usual explanations of it. The new instinct of incredulity can be rooted only in a new surmise, shared by the vulgar and the cultured alike, that we are lost. And we are lost ultimately because our world is endless. Our immersion in the things around us, our passion for science and technology, our preoccupation with production and politics, our hectic attachment to particular objects of knowledge or power, all these which make up the "secular spirit," are effects rather than causes of atheism in our time. Like atheism itself, they are the several transmutations of the new despair of man in his world.

4. THE GREAT DISAPPOINTMENT

a. *The Machine and the Void*

The modern man's love of goods and power provided by his machines is the infatuation of a jilted lover. Man's first love is life itself. If he has abandoned himself into the arms of the lifeless things he himself has made, it is because he lives in despair of his destiny in the void of his world. But, this wedding of incompatibles, of the living and of the dead, is a terrible thing. Men wedded to machines are attached to things which are absolutely alien to their own existence. Neither God nor nature blessed this union. It was simply a case of desperate man running into the arms of a painted hussy. She was very alluring. No doubt about it. She was extremely rich and talked of treasures and pleasures passing all imagination. She cooed about comfort, freedom, security, power, and everything good and lovely. But she did not understand her husband. It never occurred to her that he might care for something other than her goods; that he might have come to her not in love but in despair. Knowing nothing about life or lifetime, she thought power and goods were all a man could possibly want. She did not even suspect the existence of the other woman, man's first love, that is, life herself. She had no idea that the good a man wants is other than the goods she dangled before his eyes, or that the power she offered him might only increase his despair. So, she went on winking and boasting, being certain that she "had her man," and had him "for keeps."

But it soon became evident that the union was not quite satisfactory. Man developed a strange illness. For all the world, he acted as one poisoned. The more he lived on his woman's bounty, the worse he became. He had everything to make him happy, and he became thoroughly miserable. Instead of living in peace and security, he quarrelled endlessly and flirted with death. He was attached to his goods, but he seemed unable to enjoy them. Instead, he was busy adding more and more to what he already had, and using his goods as though they were so much trash. Every so often, he seemed to want things for no reason at all. He seemed to enjoy getting them, if "enjoy" is the word for it. But he did not even enjoy getting them. He would squander any amount of goods for some reason not good enough to satisfy a fool. A closer look made it evident that what he really wanted was to dominate. The one thing he seemed to want above all else, no matter what his profession or even his intention, was to have the power to do as he pleased. That seemed in truth to satisfy him. Whenever he had his way, one could see a strange light in his eyes, as though he had at last satisfied himself. Nobody knew where this light came from. But it was suspected that now he was mad.

Man's present infatuation with machines is unintelligible apart from their lostness in the modern world. His life without hope and his present attachment to goods made by machines are two foci of the same ellipse upon which he is enacting the *dance macabre* of contemporary life. The man of today, who has turned his machines into instruments of chaos is not merely a victim of miscalculation. He is not a child who has yet to learn the proper use of his toys. He is a desperate human being engaged in an irrational attempt to find a substitute for life itself. Machines are not simply sources of power and pleasure. They are the modern man's solution to the problem of his existence. When the good is identified with goods and power fulfills a man's life, the problem of life is solved. The insoluble problem of the good becomes changed into a multitude of soluble problems.

The ultimate function of the machine is to make man at home in his boundless world. It is supposed to give man a power which shall nullify the power of death. It is supposed to turn man into a god who shall live alone and like it. In short, the machine is proposed and accepted as the antidote to despair in the modern world.

Man's infatuation with his machines is a futile attempt at escape from his lostness in the modern world. This alone explains the strange discrepancy between his technological ingenuity and his fatal inaptitude with his fellowmen. How the same men can be at once so infernally clever and so abysmally stupid defies explanation in terms of nature and reason. It is absurd to look to human nature for an explanation of modern man's flirtations with chaos while peace and prosperity beckon to him at every corner. There is no correspondence between man's ignorance and his courting of calamity. Man's natural reason is not so deficient that it shall lead him to perambulate at the edge of destruction, yea, even walk on one foot while at it, acting for all the world as though he were very much drunk. Man's misuse of his machines suggests a radical insanity, a desperation which leads him to pursue death even while he does his best to keep alive.

Man's alienation from life and his zeal for power over all things are two sides of his existence without hope and without joy. The modern man's passion to disembowel the universe of its secrets and to exercise absolute power over nature, even at the risk of self-destruction, contains an element of lust which is not explicable except as due to a despair turned into indifference. Knowledge is good and power is good. Curiosity is good and activity is good. But lust for knowledge and lust for power as found among us are corruptions born of despair. No wonder that our "age of science" is also an age of insane and wanton destruction. Of course, "science" is not responsible for our madness. But our business is not with "science." It is with men who are bent upon rationalizing the total life of mankind. These men exist isolated in the world. Their isolation, their obsession with technics, and their lust for power are compounded into an insanity which is the undoing of nations and peoples in our time.

b. *Irrelevant Science*

The knowledge and power and goods yielded by science and technology are the most effective facts in modern life. Hence, men's reliance upon science and technics is, so to speak, a new instinct, an unquestionable conviction dominating human existence and activity in our time. This faith in science is inspired and constantly confirmed by its achievements. The scientific method is responsible for the new power of man over nature. It has given us electricity which has revolutionized our society. It has made for incredible progress in the cure and prevention of disease. It has made for new goods which are now indispensable to happiness. It is, in short, the source of "the American standard of life" which is universally acknowledged as the best thing on earth. Besides, the knowledge and power derived from science give the human spirit a new and godlike dignity. Modern science is man's crowning achievement, and men's faith in it is as reasonable as it is unquestioning.

It is now a dogma that the only way to the good life is "the scientific method." The same objectivity, the same kind of knowledge, the same skill at solving problems and adjusting parts one to another, which produced our technical civilization, are expected to bring men and groups of men together for a universal prosperity. Every other man is convinced that if he only knew the facts, all the important facts, about this economic and political problem, and if he were clever enough to comprehend the problem, he could solve it to everybody's satisfaction. He is convinced that the whole difficulty lies in the enormity and complexity of the problems confronting him. He assumes that all our perplexities and miseries and failures are due to our ignorance and inability to manage a bewilderingly involved situation: always an objective situation even though it may also involve him. So he labors and hopes against hope that he will overcome his ignorance and master his problems. He has an un-uttered and unutterable suspicion that he may never get there. If he knows enough, he knows that what he does not know is an ocean and that he cannot chart it well enough for safe sailing. But, what else is there to do? He goes on with his work.

There are indications that the problem of the good society cannot be solved by an extension of the objectifying method of the sciences to the realm of human relations. But nothing less than the ruin of our civilization will persuade our "scientific minded age" to admit that it is on the wrong track. This inertia is not due only to bad logic and bad temper. The obvious retort to the suggestion of the insufficiency of science is, What else is there? Lost men have no one but themselves. Take away their faith in themselves, faith which appears amply justified by "scientific progress," then they are absolutely lost and their despair is ultimate. In the "world of modern science" faith in the "objective method of science" is men's only ground for hope; when this faith is called in question we arrive at the limits of human despair.

Still, our situation is precarious enough to force us to doubt the suitableness of "the scientific method" for a proper handling of social problems. There is every reason for suspecting that "science" as the means of achieving peace and security among men is not only inadequate but also misleading and in principle absurd. Human relations have become "rationalized" as never before. Men do not allow much to stand in the way of their pursuit of "a good life," and they know how to attain it better than any generation before us. But the fact is that the more rationalized life becomes, the more men become irrational.

Our present faith in science is a counsel of despair. If we will not so much as look for another way to minimize the evils in our world, it is because we have no expectation of finding one. Our isolation in the modern world has convinced us that our hope to see good is in our ingenuity, that is, in science and technology. Nevertheless, we have to acknowledge that "the scientific method" has provided us with no effective antidote to the lust in our world. The reason for this failure is that our distemper is neither physical nor psychological. It originates in our relation not to things but to destiny. Science which gives us mastery over things is futile for self-mastery as we exist in relation to our metaphysical end. To rely upon it for the purification of our lust is to engage in hocus-pocus. We should not, therefore, be surprised when in spite of all sound knowledge and skill in which we excel, we can neither turn away from the road to ruin nor slow down our rush toward it. Antidote to lust must be sought in a new orientation toward destiny and this is a matter of wisdom and not of our science.

CHAPTER VII

The Problem of Love

1. *A NEW CONSPIRACY OF SILENCE*

THE NEW ENLIGHTENMENT dictates that we keep silent about death. Our intellectual leaders seem to have arrived at a tacit agreement among themselves that death is neither illuminating nor important. It is important that life is a "struggle for existence"; but it is not important that the living die. It is obvious that men work and labor in order to keep body and soul together; but they should not care that one day there shall be neither body nor soul. A man must love life; that is natural. But a man must not hate dying; that is not natural! Concern with finitude is foolish. To think of "mutability" is sentimental and in bad taste. To anticipate ultimate frustration is unintelligent and unhealthy. Gone is the Greek and Roman superstition that life is a preparation for death. Plato, the Psalmists, Buddha, the Apostle Paul, Marcus Aurelius, Augustine, Shakespeare, Donne, Pascal, Spinoza, Carlyle, Melville, Dostoevski—these and others like them, were, oh well, great men, but, then, in so far as they worried their heads about "mutability," they lacked somewhat of the good sense which makes it obvious that death has nothing to do with the way one lives.

There were times when men spoke of death with dignity and power. They faced death habitually and with an unspeakable seriousness; and they allowed it to teach them wisdom, and to make them "great." Without these men, there would have been no Western culture. Without their thoughts and perceptions, nothing in the history of Western culture is intelligible. Such men shaped the spirit of the Western world and gave it a soul without which its body is in peril of extinction . . . It has now become wisdom to ignore man's finitude and a mark of superiority to scorn anyone who so much as dares whisper the word "death." Preachers say nothing about our end, and theologians boast that they are not concerned with "physical death." Philosophers have given up preparing us for death, and our wise men teach us to forget it.

People today will not think about death and they will not talk about it. It does not concern them. They no longer care. So be it. They pay the "mortician" a thousand dollars for creating the illusion that a dead man is merely sleeping. They paint and powder the corpse. They dress him up as though he were going to a party. And why do they give him a ride such as he never had while he was alive? Why do they surround the casket with piles of gaudy flowers, and why do they cover up the grave with them? People will not speak about death. They try to cover it up by not talking about it; and when it arrives, by pretending that it is not there. But, what are all this conspiracy of silence and all this turning the other way, but dread turned into a new despair? It is despair that makes men to shut up about death. If they do not care, that also is despair. Brooding, wailing, and otherwise "carrying on" about death may become undignified and disgusting. On the other hand, to live as though there were no death is a lying life and abysmally stupid. It is the first guilt and the deadliest thing in this world. And there is no explanation for so shocking an ignorance except that it is self-imposed because of a new despair.

2. THE PROBLEM OF CONVERSATION: OF ISOLATION

Death is a macabre subject, and one would suppose that by ignoring it, men would become healthy minded and open one to another. Without the dread of death, men ought to be free from anxiety and despair. They should become extraverts and find no difficulty in communicating with their fellowmen. After all, for minds which are not related to nonbeing, everything is objective, at least virtually objective; hence, there should be no serious problem of communication. But, the facts belie such a supposition. Communication between persons has become almost impossible. One cannot converse with people any more. They will not speak to you. They do not hear what you say. You speak; they speak; but there is neither speech nor hearing. You dare not tell your friend about anything that is "personal." And if you do, you will find that he will not listen to you. So you talk about something. You rush through the how-do-you-do and fine-thank-you and how-are-you, and start a patter about the weather, prices, the noise, hard times, the world situation, etc. But all that is rather tedious. You cannot be at it for long—half-an-hour at the most. So, you propose a game of cards and a little drink. Or, you go somewhere and do something together.

Why will people not enter into conversation? Because they will not say what is on their minds, because they know that their neighbor is in no mood to listen. Men who are anxious, whose souls have tasted of despair, will neither speak their thoughts nor expect to be heard if they do it. Despair turns people into deaf-mutes. It shuts life to life and makes each man a stranger to his neighbor. But, what is this despair which makes communication between persons so difficult and almost hopeless? It cannot be despair about health, or property, or friends. Such problems are usually far from desperate. They are common problems which ought to interest one's friends and make communication with them helpful. The despair which shuts the mouths of men and makes them talk drivel is not despair with anything in particular. It is the despair of life itself. It is a repressed and dumbfounding despair which condemns men to solitude and loneliness. Hence it is that there is so much talk and so little understanding.

Men are huddled together, and each one is alone. They spend billions in order to be in some sort of a crowd. They can no longer abide being alone. They cannot resist busy thoroughfares, restaurants, stadiums, movie houses, clubs, lodges, churches, lecture halls, etc. Anywhere they walk in, they want to see someone smile at them and call them by their first name. They are pathetically eager to be fussed over and guffawed with. Hence they huddle together so much that they are continually getting on one another's nerves and falling apart. They fall apart so easily because they seldom get together as persons. In the crowd, a man is not a person. His private life is excluded from his participation in the life of the group. After all, the main function of the group is to divert him, to take him away from himself. Hence it is only fair that he should get lost in it. But, in this self-repudiation, he is desperately alone.

The pathetic eagerness of men today to go some place, to be in a crowd, to do something, is born of loneliness, of an inner emptiness which is the counterpart of the void around them. In fact, the group can do nothing but divert attention from this prior misery which drives men to it. It diverts attention, but in so doing it establishes the despair in the soul; for now there is no escape from the wasteland without and the desert within. When men in despair huddle together they are not thereby comforted. They in fact irritate one another. This also is an evidence of the despair in the new world.

3. *THE CONGESTED WORLD*

Men, other than astronomers and a few dreamers, do not spend their time staring at the endless spaces. This is just as well. The eyes were placed upon the forehead because they are meant to look upon the fullness of the earth and not upon the emptiness of the heavens. Men are completely immersed in their thousand terrible problems all over the earth. Who cares whether the world be bounded or unbounded? Our anxieties, dreads, despairs are social and not spatial. There are good and well-known reasons why men are crowded together and lonely in our world: good social and psychological reasons. Men are preoccupied with men and not with the universe. Hence, the universe has nothing to do with the matter.

Still, why has the earth become so small and so congested? Why cannot men keep from stepping upon one another's toes, even though they may be walking upon a fairly wide street? Why do they keep brushing against one another, apologizing, growling, and going their way? The world has shrunk to the size of a tiny Polynesian island. It is no longer big enough for all the people who live on it. Each man is worried that there will not be room enough for himself, and is constantly pushing with both elbows. He is watchful lest he be thrown into the water. He is so busy keeping his foothold that he cannot so much as turn his eyes to the sea. He even forgets that he is on an island. His life is so full of problems to be solved, and so infested with dangers to be overcome, that it takes all the wit and energy he has in order to attend to these, without spending himself in futile contemplation of the sea about him.

Quite so. Nevertheless, he does not escape his situation by forgetting about it. He remains lost, and his lostness conditions his hectic existence. Men who despair of escape from a tiny island may be very busy bickering and quarreling among themselves. But still, it would be impossible to understand the whole of their unwholesome existence, without taking into account that they *are lost, and without hope.*

So it is with the man in the modern world. His continuous failures to live intelligently and decently, his neuroses and psychoses, his self-contradictions in thought and act, his pathetic grasping for life and happiness, and his constant toying with death and lapses into abysmal misery—these have their proximate social and psychological explanations. One can make economic, political, technological, moral, historical, educational, studies of our complicated common life. One can discuss capitalism, communism, totalitarianism, democracy, values and traditions, etc. One can point out that the earth has shrunk through our means of communication and that our institutions have become too big because of our technological and industrial advances. One can go on endlessly, and elaborately, with problems of this "one world" and show how they are all but insoluble. But if one forgets that we are lost in our world, one cannot understand our existence today.

The panic of the Western man today is inexplicable in terms of his acknowledged problems. One is not absolutely helpless. Actually, there is space enough to enable anyone to move away a bit, and to mitigate any pressure one does not like. One can contrive a bit, and resist a bit, and have some hope of success toward a decent life. It is irrational and cowardly to despair in relation to men and institutions. Nevertheless, we do despair, even though we are not cowards. We despair because the relative frustrations of life in our society are occasions for the quickening of an absolute frustration in the human soul.

Our personal and social problems are vehicles of our metaphysical despair with our existence. Hence they are endowed with a seriousness incommensurate with the relative good or evil they embody. In themselves, they are of relative difficulty; but as tokens of the peril of life itself, they are unmanageable. It is precisely in the problems of "daily bread" and security that we meet the ultimate problem of life itself; our chronic failure to deal intelligently with problems of daily existence is the primary evidence of our despair in our world.

4. *OF SELF-PITY, SELF-HATRED, PITY, AND CALLOUSNESS*

The man in an empty world is a terrible egotist. The public world being empty, he fancies a private world of his own. He fills the latter with images torn from the outer world and invests them with all of his frustrated vitality. These images are endowed with feeling and sensibility. They fuse with his soul and inflate it. They produce an inner world of being and becoming which is apart from the empty world outside, and replaces it. Here he is secure against the void. Here, he is the lord of a world of his own. Everything in his world is his own. In fact, it is he himself who is everything in this inner world. Hence, he is extremely partial to the goings on within. His emotions are the very stuff of his life, and his inner hurts are threats to his very existence. Although on this side of insanity, he knows the inner world as one of shadows and make-believe, he clings to it as the only sure thing in this world of vanities and resists every threat to the ego which rules over it.

The "ego" is a pretense, and the egotist knows this. He is not foolish enough to believe that the world inside is the real world, or that its *plenum* fills up the emptiness of the public world in which he in fact exists. Hence, even while he builds up his self-world, he is frustrated and lives in bitterness. He hates the nothing he creates out of nothing. His self-love which is his love of life in the public world, is turned into self-hatred; and he rebels against the world and everything in it. The selfish man who has tasted of despair (and who has not done so?) corrupts his natural self-love into self-hatred, and lives without joy even while he posits himself and asserts himself against every one else.

Natural self-love informed by reason is an indispensable element in any ongoing society. It is the impulse to live and to enjoy things. Even the "selfishness" in self-love is an inevitable consequence of the fact that human beings cannot feel another's good as they do their own. But the "selfishness" that goes with self-assertion is a radically different matter. It is born of self-hatred. The selfish man does not enjoy the goods he has or lusts after. What he has is not good; and what he has not, he wants not because he loves it but because he is loveless. He does not love his good. He does not love himself. He in fact hates himself; and with himself, he hates his neighbor.

The self-hatred in selfishness is unbearable. Hence it is readily transmuted into self-pity. The hated self is objectified into the pitied self. Moral revulsion is replaced by the esthetic, and the self-hater contemplates himself as a pitiful soul caught in a spiky net of misfortune. But self-pity also is unbearable. The self-objectification in it is not enough to free a man from the despair in his soul. Hence, the man who pities himself seeks others who may become objects of his pity. He looks for and finds evidences of misery in others, and pities them with the selfsame pity with which he pities himself. He is especially partial to infants and little beasts who, in their helpless suffering, are perfect objectifications of self-pity.

The objects of self-pity are extremely prone to ingratitude, and even to rudeness and rebellion. They become unaccountably sullen, uncooperative and even defiant. They are either too obsequious or too "fresh," either too self-effacing or too self-asserting. They are strangely difficult and unpredictable. The selfsame despair which informs the pity of the powerful, makes the weak petulant. The self-hatred of the inferior, as that of the superior, is changed readily into self-pity. But self-pity in this case has no outlet in pity-full acts. Such outlet wanting, self-pity reverts to self-hatred and an envious hatred of those who have the power to do good.

Western society today is a hotbed of self-pity. Lonely men, severally in despair, have developed a sentiment of community which is at once soft and callous. It is as though they were inmates in a hospital for incurables. There is a great deal of mutual sighing: "That fellow is worse off than I am," "I am dreadfully sorry," "Oh, how it must hurt, I wish I could help you." No matter how much of a brave front these inmates may put up, no matter how much "fun" they may have, they are without hope and without joy. Each man pities the others. But he pities himself in a special way. In fact, he sometimes does not care one whit whether the next fellow is dead or alive. He feels with his fellow inmates, and he does not feel with them at all. He cares for them, and he does not care at all. His caring and not caring alike are not so much responses as eruptions. They correspond not so much to his neighbor's situation, as to the workings of the misery within him. They weave their senseless patterns without regard to reason or right, inducing a kind of hospital madness upon the sanest patient in the place: a madness characterized by the contradictory workings of pity and callousness in the same sick soul. A sick man has a lot of feeling for the miserable fellows around him. Nevertheless, he is a sick man and not a saint. And it is very dangerous for our common life that the difference between these two is all but unknown.

The pitying soul suppresses its pity and turns callous. The willing callousness of such a person is other than a lack of imagination. It is the suppression of the imagination by one who projects his despair into his duty. He is neither as helpless nor as sensible as he pretends. There is no objective ground for the sense of sheer futility in his soul. The objective situation is not simply desperate. It may be very difficult, and almost desperate. But, a man can do *something:* which is better than nothing. Callousness, moreover, cannot be explained in terms of self-love and the struggle for existence. There is no natural limitation or animal impulse that can account for the bitterness in the hard heart of man. Callousness is despair in disguise. It is the desperate man's means of doing away with the self-pity poisoning him and taking away his joy. It is the triumph of the void in one's own soul, making all relations empty and turning life itself into a foretaste of death.

5. *THE PROBLEM OF LOVE*

This callousness goes with a terrible desire for love or sympathy. The new alienation of man from his world makes him to cling to his fellowmen with a determined fervor. Being left alone with his fellowmen, he exists in a new and absolute dependence upon them. He lives with a new conviction that weal and woe depend upon the help or hindrance he shall receive from those around him. Hence, his desire for love and cooperation becomes a matter of life and death.

The love of one's fellowmen has become the deepest need of our time. A man is almost beside himself when he finds a friend who is a "real pal" and "will do anything for him." Nothing in the world could induce him to cross his friend and even to offend him. He cares neither for truth nor for right so long as he can please his friend. He will help him at the expense of anybody else and will remain to him a loyal friend come what may. Thus he would like a friend to love him and thus he himself must love a friend.

Yes, indeed! Love is a great thing, the greatest thing in the world. The poets and the preachers say so; and they are right. Everybody knows that personal, social, international problems, which are driving us mad, cannot be solved without love. The psychologists will tell you that you will have no peace unless you love people and people love you. Social reformers will tell you that unless capital and labor, Jews and Gentiles, the colored people and the uncolored, learn to understand, and love, and trust one another, there is not much hope for anybody. Those who talk and write about group relations will tell you that unless the nations learn to understand, and love, and trust one another, we shall all come to a terrible end.

Alas, it has become just as hard to love as to live without love. Everyone who loves love knows how hard it is to love one's fellowmen. It is one thing to want love and quite another to have it and to give it. There is something inside of us that makes the openness and generosity of love out of the question. The soul of every man is shut up to the soul of every other man. It has its own private despair with its destiny, its own knowledge of its own lostness, its own devastating resentment of its own nullifying fate. It anticipates its ultimate separation from the society of men in a virtual but all too real separation from them even now. Men used to say that every man must one day meet his God alone. The modern man is convinced that he must one day meet the void alone. Hence, he lives alone, that is, he lives without love.

The despair in the modern man makes love at once imperative and impossible. Hence, he is at once frustrated and guilty. He is unable to love and is consistently blamed for his lovelessness. The demand for love is categorical and irresistible. Loving, on the other hand, is a "moral impossibility." The universal assumption of the other man's guilt is not an accident. There is an open secret that love is no less rare than it is right.

Hence lust for power has assumed a new virulence among us. Modern "technology" has been an overwhelming temptation for lust among both men and nations. But the manufactory of lust is in the souls of men who live without hope.

CHAPTER VIII

Antidote to Lust

1. *LOVE FOR LIFE*

LUST IS CORRUPTED LOVE. It is love corrupted, as we
have seen, by despair with one's destiny. This despair turns
one's natural love for his being into an abhorrence and a revulsion. It now becomes an irresistible temptation to turn away
from the void which threatens one's existence, and to preoccupy
oneself with goods which are available as well as enjoyable.
But such preoccupation is characterized by a lack of measure
and proportion. Every other good draws us to itself as if it were
the absolute good. We pursue our objectives with a passion
which has nothing to do with the amount of good in them.
Goods promise us a good which they cannot yield for the simple
reason that they do not contain it. Every attainment becomes a
frustration confirming the despair in us and pushing us back
into the void in which we exist. Thus it is that, instead of
enjoying the solid satisfactions of love, we are subjected to the
endless frustrations of lust, and we live without good and without joy. In such a life, power itself, which is the means of good
and joy, becomes their substitute, and lust for power replaces
the love of life itself.

Love for life is the only authentic antidote to lust in general and to lust for power in particular.

Love for life is not exuberance of a healthy animal. It is
neither natural nor possible for man to exist as the flowers of
the field or the birds of the air, even though he may be inspired
by them. To be human is to exist in one's lifetime and under
the shadow of the void. To love life, for us, is to acknowledge

this shadow under which we exist. It is to confront the void discerned through the shadow, and not to turn away from the darkness overhanging it. Whatever our temperament, to love life is to cry out from the depths against a destiny which is to us the removal of the condition of all good. It is an intelligence and singleness of mind which comprehends that neither possessions, nor prestige, nor security, nor knowledge, nor power, is good except to one who is alive. It is to be possessed of a simplicity of heart which enables us to exist in the truth that there is no substitute for our being. To love life is to resist the most bewildering of all confusions, that is, the confusion of being with having.

The love of life is that wisdom whereby we "number our days." It is to acknowledge that our lifetime, the time which is the measure of our lives, has a beginning and an end. It is to remember the past and to anticipate the future, and to be properly impressed with the fact that they both issue in the void. It is to set the cut off time of our existence over against that endless time during which we do not exist. It is to exist in time, and to repudiate the self-repudiation of an existence in which everything is temporal except the human being who desires or enjoys it. Since for man to be is to be in time, the love of being is to refuse to be lost in the times of other beings. It is to number one's own days, and to relate all times to the time of one's own being. To love life is to join time and space together, to love life and goods together, and to allow the love of life to qualify the love of goods. To love life is to love all goods *sub specie vitae*. It is to number one's days while one numbers one's goods. The difference between a wise man and a fool is that the former numbers his days, and the latter will not do it. The difference between a human being and a brute of a man is that the former exists in his lifetime and the latter is always moving away from it. The man loves life and enjoys his goods accordingly; the brute despises life and lusts after "goods," turning good into evil and life into death.

To love life is to know despair, and to know despair is to

know guilt. As it is impossible to love life without despair, so it is impossible to despair without being guilty. The love of life expresses itself in a sobriety and an accompanying humility which were foolish unless a man exist in guilt. It is an inane face that registers pleasure or pain without also revealing a serious soul, that is, a soul which has tasted of despair and guilt. The expression of authentic humanity is a unique and strange light which is also a gloom, a gloom which is also light. This gloom-light is a matter of fate and freedom, of despair and guilt, in which one man sees another in understanding and love, and is united with him "in the bundle of life." An empty face is the face of a man who exists as though he were a "babe in arms," laughing and crying indifferently to the despair and guilt in him. Such a face is devoid of that beauty and dignity which is peculiar to the human being. It lacks light and intelligence. It is a face without love and without power. It is a void; death itself staring us in the face. A man without an awareness of the mystery of guilt within his soul is one whose despair has already destroyed his love of being and has, with it, incapacitated him for love toward his fellowmen.

To love life is to obey the commandment, "Thou shalt love thy neighbor as thyself." It is to love oneself and one's neighbor as human beings, as those with the same fate and the same freedom, tempted at all times to despair because of their fate, to hate their common life and therewith one another. To love life is to acknowledge the wrong in the lust which makes us to turn against ourselves and against our neighbor. It is to set aside all subterfuge and self-justification, and to confess our guilt in that we do not love our neighbor as ourselves. It is that humility among men which begs for understanding and forgiveness. It joins all men in prayer for "faith" which shall purify our lust and restore us to that love which shall bind us together in compassion and justice.

2. *THE AMBIGUITY OF EXISTENCE*

The strange but inescapable fact is that in human existence despair and guilt are joined together. This fact is strange because it appears illogical. If the destiny of man is the void, it is right, and therefore, not guilty, to despair. If it is in fact guilty to despair, then the void is a delusion and we ought not to despair. It cannot be at once right and guilty to despair. But despair *is* at once right and guilty; or, despair is at once wrong and reasonable.

During the ages of faith, men acknowledged their guilt and their despair issued from their sense of guilt. Their primary concern was "eternal death" in hell. In this our time, men take the void for granted, and live in despair. They live for the enjoyment of available goods (which is a form of despair), and all the while plead "not guilty." Believers acknowledge guilt but repudiate despair. Unbelievers may or may not acknowledge despair, but they certainly repudiate guilt. Such are the alternatives before the mind: belief or unbelief, guilt or despair.

Still, the fact is that lust is the joint product of both guilt and despair. Neither guilt alone, nor despair alone, can turn love into lust. The guilty believer lives in the hope of forgiveness; and forgiveness restores him to love and justice. The desperate unbeliever is overwhelmed by the vanity of life, and succumbs to an apathy which is the end of love and lust alike. Lust does not flourish in one who is either simply guilty or simply desperate. But lust is a universal fact. Therefore men exist ambiguously as at once possessed of both despair and guilt. The lust in the believer means that, contrary to his opinion of himself, he is a man of despair. The same lust in the unbeliever means that in spite of his conviction of innocence, he exists as one who is guilty. In fact, the guilt of the believer is a product of his despair, and the despair of the unbeliever is a product of his guilt.

Human life, and the works of man, are unintelligible apart from the fact that in us despair and guilt work together as the double engine which is the source of the boundless infernal energy making for the desolations upon the earth. The erstwhile predominance of the sense of guilt in Christendom was a natural consequence of a common faith under the tutelage of the churches. Men who took for granted an eternal existence in heaven or hell, took guilt as their major problem and sought a righteousness which would see them to heaven, or at least to purgatory. On the other hand, the despair of the modern man is a natural consequence of the removal of heaven and hell from the map of his world. Since the righteous and the wicked alike end in the void, guilt has no ultimate cosmic significance. But still, lust has prevailed in Christendom, and continues to prevail. And the only illuminating explanation of this fact is that, in spite of both belief and unbelief, guilt is qualified by despair and despair by guilt. A man may, in his mind, be a believer; still, he exists in despair producing guilt and in guilt producing despair. A man may, in his mind, be an unbeliever; still, he exists in guilt producing despair and in despair producing guilt. The believer may be unaware of his despair, and the unbeliever of his guilt. But since both of them are possessed of lust, they exist ambiguously, related at once to the eternal and the void. And this ambiguous existence is the source of a faith which is prior to both belief and unbelief.

It is the fate of the modern man to live with a decisive apprehension of the void. The temptation to despair comes to us with a new power in the "world of modern science." No sophistry nor evasion can alter our existence in "an infinity of worlds." The "perfect world" of the Middle Ages is gone. Traditional supernaturalism has become alien to the modern thought and imagination. The existence of heaven above and hell below has become all but incredible. In spite of the embarrassment of our imaginations, we have become virtually convinced in our minds that the setting of our existence is an infinite void. Hence, we exist under a shadow beyond which we see only darkness. Men who lived in a finite world imagined that they saw the eternal. We who live in the new and "infinite" world, see the void and not the eternal. Man's apprehension of the void has attained a new clarity; hence the despair in his soul has become explicit and overwhelming in a new way.

Nevertheless, the void we see offers us no authentic explanation of the guilt and despair in our souls. We cannot avoid the suspicion that our despair is a matter of emotion rather than intelligence, and that our denial of guilt is itself a guilty evasion. Even though we see the void, we are not thereby justified in thinking and living by sight alone. The void we see explains neither our despair nor our guilt. Despair can arise only from a hope frustrated, and guilt makes sense only in an existence in relation to the eternal. There is no guilt without faith and no despair without hope. The void cannot evoke either faith or hope. Therefore, we exist ambiguously, so that the shadow under which we see the void is cast by the eternal which alone can be the source of both faith and hope.

We shall neither understand our lust nor find an antidote to it, unless we exist under the shadow and think accordingly. The time has come, as it were, "to get hold of ourselves." Neither the superstitions of the believers nor the denials of the unbelievers will any longer do. Both belief and unbelief are futile and maddening efforts to move away from the shadow which requires that we live and act by faith. Did we live in light without darkness, there would be no shadow, nor despair nor guilt. Did we live in darkness without light, there would again be no shadow, and again neither despair nor guilt. Belief without unbelief and unbelief without belief, rather, belief and unbelief alike are excluded; because we exist under a shadow which reveals both light and darkness. We see the darkness, but we exist by faith. Faith is not sight; hence, credulity is foolish. But, there is no sight without faith; hence, unbelief is equally foolish.

We see the void, but we live by faith. It is not possible to exist as a human being, that is, to exist rationally, without discriminating between goods and taking some matters seriously. We may think that good and evil are unreal, and we may refuse to think that anything is serious. But we cannot help having contempt for a man who lives as though there were no difference between good and evil and for one "who cannot be serious." Truth and lies, justice and injustice, love and neglect, are real opposites, and the difference between them is a serious matter. One's work, and freedom, and security, and social responsibilities are similarly serious. A man must be serious. He must not be a loiterer, a pretender, a windbag, an incompetent or a quack. Existence is serious, and the void itself cannot turn it into a joke. Even a clown must take his job seriously. He must be a passionate funster. Otherwise he is a fool, and even fools boo him off the stage.

It is the ambiguity of existence that makes human life a serious matter. If man knew himself as immortal, he could not take the present life seriously. The more credulous people are, the less serious they are. Their security turns their religion and their lives into mere ritual. The superstitious have a minimum of authentic faith. On the other hand, the more certain a man is of his unbelief and therefore the more hopeless concerning his destiny, the more he must be impressed with the ultimately inconsequential nature of his life and works, and the less serious he also becomes. After all, nothing inconsequential can be real, or serious. Hence, neither our immortality nor our mortality, as matters of certain knowledge, explains the serious character of the human enterprise. It is human and right to be serious, as it is inhuman and wrong not to be serious, because we exist ambiguously in darkness and in light.

Seriousness itself is ambiguous. A serious man takes himself seriously, and he does not take himself seriously. He is a man of passion, but also he has "a sense of humor." He is passionate without being fanatical, disinterested without being indifferent. He acts as though his decisions were for life and death. Still, he knows that there is only one matter of life and death, and that is existence itself. He lives in a vacuum, and yet his world is full of substantial entities. Everything is vanity; nevertheless, nothing is in vain. The serious man lives in the tension of these opposites. But strangely enough, this same tension is the source of his sense of proportion. It enables him to distinguish between greater and lesser goods; and what is decisive, to live according to the distinctions he makes. The serious man alone is a wise man, and can alone achieve a human or rational existence.

The life of man in the depths is ambiguous. There are indeed habitual responses, prevailing attitudes, clear ideas, concrete choices, discrete emotions, and the rest. But the agent himself is in a state of radical ambiguity. He exists as an ambiguous source of both good and evil. He intends the good; he mixes his good intention with evil; he intends both good and evil at the same time. He intends good, and is repelled by it. He is repelled by evil, and yet fascinated and attracted by it. The good is dreadful, and evil is gratifying, or at least "interesting." Such is the ambiguity of our relationships to good and evil. If we acknowledge this ambiguity, and exist accordingly, we fulfill the first condition of a rational existence and are enabled to choose the good and to eschew evil. If we deny this ambiguity, everything becomes confusion. We intend the good, and perpetrate evil. We intend evil pretending that we intend the good, and again we perpetrate evil. Goods come to us posing as evil, and evils come posing as good. Our sense of proportion deteriorates. The better appears as the worse and the worse as better. We are continually mistaken and continually disappointed. Sound judgment in matters of good and evil is a function of faith, that is, of a firm comprehension of our existence as ambiguous.

The ambiguity of existence finds perennial expression in the ambiguities of human motives. When we meet a man who thinks that he is motivated simply and clearly by altruism, or a common good, we suspect that we are dealing with either a hypocrite, or a fool, or both. If we are wise, we shall not be surprised if he next shows utmost indifference for the welfare of any one but himself. When we meet a man who wants nothing but peace, or freedom, or security, or the friendship of his fellowmen, we must not be surprised if the fellow turns out to be one who wants his way at the expense of peace, freedom, and all other good. In fact, when we come across one who knows what he wants and what he does not want, and that certainly and with a single mind, we must be prepared to have met a boor and a bore. This man has an unambiguous knowledge not only of himself but also of his neighbor. That man knows what is right, and that he is right and another is wrong. The third man whose intentions are always of the best, drives relentlessly until they are realized. Leave them alone. You may not expect wisdom from them, and much less humility and respect for their fellowmen. They are fanatics who live on lies and the flesh and blood of their neighbors. When men lose sight of the ambiguities of their motives, they are full of contradictions. They become miserymakers.

The world of things is ideally unambiguous. We know the things in it when we "have their number," and what is numerical is unambiguous. It is the function of science to remove the ambiguities in our perceptions and to resolve the contradictions in our ideas of things. Thus men attain a true knowledge of the "external world," and with it they acquire the power essential for civilization. Such is not the case in the world of persons. The ambiguity of human existence, and the consequent ambiguities of human motives, cannot be removed. They can only be ignored. And when they are ignored, the life of man is turned into a jungle of contradictions. The more we rely upon our knowledge of ourselves and others as objects, the more we become unpredictable and bewildering. The more human life is "rationalized," the more irrational it becomes. The more we are taken in by "human engineering," the more unreliable and unmanageable human relations become. It is, therefore, not surprising that this "age of science" is also "the age of anxiety." The denial of ambiguity turns men into neurotics. The truth is that our existence *is* ambiguous; we live in a light that is gloom, and in a gloom that is light. The first principle of a natural existence for man is to live by this truth.

3. *CIVILIZATION AND CULTURE*

There are two kinds of truth, and two kinds of intelligence corresponding to them. The first is the truth about things, expressed ultimately in the clarifications and formulae of mathematical science. Such truth is a matter of technique and skills, and gives power over the things around us. It is attained through an intelligence whose virtue it is to discover how things "work." In this sense, the intelligent man is one who is clever at counting the numbers of causes and effects and at altering numbers so as to produce new effects. He is a man who knows both what he wants and how to get it. What he wants may be knowledge, or riches, or power, or prestige. By his own lights, he may work for public welfare and progress. In any case, his mind abhors ambiguity. His own aim is to achieve clarity both in his ends and in the means he employs. And the more he knows how to achieve his ends, the more clever and the more intelligent he is. For him, truth is "operational," and his intelligence is technical.

The second kind of truth concerns the ambiguity of existence, and the intelligence which apprehends it is wisdom. Here the mind moves in a direction opposite to the one described above. It moves from clarity toward ambiguity, from certainty toward doubt, from the simple toward the complex, from the naive toward the subtle, from idea toward existence. To the wise man, the one indispensable truth, the truth of the manner of one's existence, is far from obvious. He does not live for any one end; neither does he live for any one set of discrete ends. It turns out that his ends are partial and his motives mixed. There is repeatedly a question as to whether the end justifies the means, and as to how far an end in view motivates a proposed action. The wise man knows that the human aspect of any situation is decisive for the good and evil in it, and that no technical achievement as such is good and not evil. He knows that however brilliant a technical success, the self-realization attained through it is a function of his relations to his fellowmen. But such knowledge requires a serious interest in and aptitude for

self-knowledge. It requires a sensitivity to the disparities between thought and existence in one's own life; an awareness of
impulses which are partly incongruous with one's purposes.
The clarities of thought, volition and action alike, emerge from
an ambiguous deep, and like objects retrieved from the water,
they refer us back to the sea whence they came. All ideas which
involve personal relationships are steeped in ambiguity, and it
is the essence of wisdom to acknowledge this fact. The more
discerning we become the more we are led from one ambiguity
to another, the more our minds are purified, the more we exist
in an understanding without which our humanity itself is corrupted and destroyed.

The distinction between these two kinds of truth made
above is extremely useful in distinguishing between civilization
and culture, both of which are imperilled at this time. Civilization is the outcome of ingenuity, invention, and technics. Its
progress is marked by an increasing knowledge of the "order
and connections of things," and by an increasing ability to
manipulate them towards a "more abundant life." Agriculture,
industry, transportation, building, and the economic and political institutions which make for maximum production and enjoyment, mark the extent of civilization attained by a given
society. Such enterprises are dependent upon observation, ex-
periment, formulation, and the like, which lead to "clear and
distinct ideas." Such ideas find their ultimate expressions in
mathematical symbols which represent the final dissipation of
all ambiguity. Clarity in the "knowledge of the external world"
is both the source and a major triumph of civilization.

Culture as represented especially by philosophy and art is
an entirely different matter. From Socrates down, it has been
the endless task of the philosopher to embarrass the man who
goes about with "clear and distinct ideas." The vulgar man
knows both truth and the truth of the matter, both the good and
what is good for him, both beauty and the beautiful. His five
senses give him reliable information about his world, and his
mind grasps facts firmly and adequately. His language is literal,

and his thoughts are exact replicas of the real world. And the more scientific he becomes, the more certain he becomes of truth and error, of the verified and the unverified. But when the philosopher appears on the scene, all this certainty and precision do not last for long. Of course, the symbols and the formulae remain intact. But their meaning and significance become ambiguous. One now asks: What is reality? What is a fact? And what is an object? Of course, there are so-called philosophers who think they know the answers to such questions. But the more of a philosopher a man is the less his mind coincides with the minds of others. In fact, the "greater" the philosopher, the more radical and thoroughgoing are his criticisms of other philosophers, and the more his "system" is his own and not that of someone else. Every philosopher of parts has a "smell" all his own, and his awareness of truth and reality is both unique and unrepeatable. Moreover, those who study and expound his philosophy, cannot agree among themselves as to what it was precisely that he said and meant to say. Hence, even men like Descartes and Spinoza, let alone Plato, Leibniz, Locke, Kant, William James and Whitehead, are open to various interpretations and shall be reinterpreted so long as they are known and seriously studied. There will be other "great" philosophers who will create their own more or less unified systems and their own disciples or critics who will debate endlessly as to what they really thought and said. This kind of human activity will go on without ever attaining the unequivocal certainties of knowledge acquired through scientific discipline. It is the philosopher's curious but indispensable function to expose the ambiguities in human thought, and through clarification to lead the mind of the vulgar to an awareness of the ultimate ambiguity of existence itself. Persistent and adequate critique of matters scientific, esthetic, ethical, political, leads us, as it were by the nose, to ambiguities which defy clarification and comprehension. There will be no end to definings of the good, and beautiful, and the true. There will be no end to the tensions between the universal and particular, between the abstract and the concrete, between essence and existence. Philosophy is criticism inspired by the ambiguity of existence, and its ultimate justification is its conduciveness to exist in this ambiguity. It is the love of wisdom; but the essence of wisdom is the capacity for being in every instance critical; but, moreover, man has such a capacity because he in fact exists ambiguously. Culture as expressed by philosophy is a product of wisdom, and wisdom is inspired by our ambiguous existence.

The culture of a people is conspicuous in its artistic achievements: in its literature, music, painting, sculpture, architecture, dance and drama. Here the endless reflections of wise men are matched by the endless creative work of the artists. Men in each generation are inspired by a strange impulse to produce works of "beauty" which are a joy to the human soul. Men of one "period" learn from their predecessors, and one can speak of the development of art in terms of skill and execution. But, there is no such thing as progress in the creation of beauty. Progress which is so obvious in science is extremely debatable in art. In respect to beauty, one cannot say that medieval art is inferior to modern, or that Dutch painters are inferior to Italian. One cannot say that Eugene O'Neill is a better dramatist than Shakespeare, or that Prokofieff is superior to Bach. Beauty knows neither time nor place. It is a constant, albeit ambiguous, quality which satisfies a perennial hunger and thirst of the human soul. The techniques of art can be taught; but the beauty of a work of art is evoked in the soul and must be re-evoked in every one who would "appreciate" it.

The beauty in art is not dependent upon its subject matter. It is not in the ingenuity with which its parts are put together. It is not even in the intensity of feeling it produces in us. A portrait by Bruegel may not be pretty; but it is beautiful. "Macbeth" deals with evil, but it is a beautiful play. A concerto by Saint-Saens may be very ingenious, but it is not beautiful; on the other hand, a song by Schubert is simplicity itself, and still —beautiful. Rachmaninoff arouses the emotions with music written less beautifully than a quartet by Mozart which causes in us no meaningless excitement. Criticism of a work of art reveals that both knowledge and technique have gone into its making. It reveals details which show unusual discernment and sensibility, and that an intelligence of high order has been at work in comprehension and composition. The more we notice these things, the more we admire the artist, and the more richly we are moved by his performance. But such "appreciation" is not enough. In fact, it is disappointing and even disgusting to hear music or to look at painting which is merely ingenious or emotional. Art without "something more" is not art; it is a pretense and a deception. It diverts us, but it also cheats us and leaves us empty.

The "something more" in art, or its beauty, is in the soul of the artist, and therefore in his works. But what is the "soul"? The soul is our ambiguous existence; the bearer of a light that is gloom, and of a gloom that is light. The beauty in art is essentially ambiguous, and this ambiguity is characteristic of our existence.

Art is notoriously a matter of the imagination. A man who sees and reports "bare facts" is not an artist. He may be an acute observer and a faithful reproducer, but still, he is no artist. On the other hand, a purely fanciful fellow also is not an artist. A man whose imagination breaks loose from the world in which we exist, and spends itself in building "castles in air," lacks the artist's passion for truth without which a man can neither seek nor find beauty. Art therefore is neither re-presentation or misre-presentation of facts. It is to bring facts into a living relation with the soul of man. Now, imagination is the function in which thought and existence touch one another. It is the power to apprehend the concrete or that which exists. Artistic imagination is the power to apprehend the world in the light of our own concrete and ambiguous existence. Our notion of things as existent depends upon our apprehension of ourselves as existent beings. Our own existence being ambiguous, our primary experience of the world is suffused with the strange light of our imagination which enables us to think as those who exist. This light is perceived most strikingly in portraits. But it is perceived also in every work of authentic art. It is the essence of art, that without which art is not art. The imagination with its ambiguous relationship to things and thought is the proper vehicle of the truth that we who imagine exist ambiguously, confronting a destiny which evokes both despair and hope in us. The function of art is to lure us to the shadow of an ambiguous destiny. In this way, art is no less concerned with "truth" than with beauty. "Serious" or authentic art, as against "amusement," is one in which "truth is beauty and beauty truth." But the unity of truth and beauty is only in the soul. Everywhere else, truth may be ugly and the beautiful untrue. The transcendent and undefinable "good" of Plato, the corresponding "beauty" of the artist, and the evasive but inescapable "truth" of the wise man's search, are revealed in the soul of man who exists ambiguously. Hence it is that the disciplined imagination of the artist is indispensable for our very existence as "rational creation."

Civilization depends upon our knowledge of our world. Culture depends upon our knowledge of ourselves. The former depends upon the clarification of objects and power over our environment. The latter depends upon a continual recovery of the ambiguities of our existence and the humility such recovery evokes in us. Civilization as such is a perennial source of lust, and the "higher" the civilization, the more energetic the lust. There is no single formula which explains the rise and fall of civilizations. But still, as lust in a human being marks his corruption and virtual dissolution, so lust in a society generated by the powers in it, mark its corruption, decline, and destruction. Unless a vigorous culture act as an antidote to the lusts generated by civilization, its inhumanities will lead to its death through one cause or another.

Culture is the perennial cathartic which purifies the soul of its lust and corruption. The power of music to exorcise evil spirits has been known from China to Spain. But the same power has been exercised by poetry and drama, by painting and sculpture, and by the dance. Generation after generation, in many lands, the artists have given the people joy. They have not only entertained them and made them to laugh and weep, but also they have moved them in the depths and opened their souls to an ambiguous light, making them at once serious and joyful. They have lured them back to the shadow and exposed them to its benign influence. Philosophers, famous and now unknown, have taught men wisdom, and artists have moved them to humility and love. They have thus transformed, through the ages, despair into hope, and lust into love. Culture has been a perennial antidote to lust. It has been a source of both humanity and community.

4. THE CORRUPTION OF CULTURE

However, culture itself has a strange tendency to become denatured. The more advanced the civilization, the more likely culture is to turn into sophistication and estheticism. The lust generated by the power embodied in civilization works itself into the souls of philosopher and artist alike. The former of these turns into a sophist, and the latter into an esthete. Both can no longer abide ambiguity. The philosopher passes from existence to thought and burns his bridges behind him. The dynamic tensions of thought inspired by existence are set aside in favor of an ideal, rather verbal, consistency which shall be the end of all authentic thinking. By hook and by crook, the thinker arrives at a "system" which marks the end of wisdom and humility alike. Thus philosophy becomes "academic," and ceases to illumine the common life of the people. Sooner or later, it becomes evident that authentic clarification is a scientific enterprise and that the scientist alone is qualified to systematize knowledge. Thus the philosopher is left without a reason for being, and wisdom is left without its advocate. But where there is no wisdom, there is no antidote to lust.

The artist is subject to his own peculiar temptation. He also becomes addicted to clarification; in his case the end of art becomes the clarification of the emotions. Intelligence now degenerates into skill in arousing emotion. The artist now becomes a clever fellow who can make people laugh or cry over one thing or another. He becomes adept at playing with the passions of men, stimulating their sensuous appetites, enabling them to enjoy vicariously experiences of power and luxury, luring them into the land of make-believe where everything can happen but existence itself. The chief function of art now becomes "emotional release." People go to shows and concert halls with the primary hope of feeling something. They expect the artist to excite them until they gulp and perhaps even have tears in their eyes. They expect the maestro to pull at their heart strings, to make them either to swon or to go momentarily mad in a bedlam of rhythm and noise. Of course, nobody is supposed to take either art or the artist seriously. Everybody knows that the whole thing is play-acting. Everybody knows that there is no connection between art and existence, and that the newspapers list music and the theatre alike under "amusements." "Rationalized" existence in civilized societies threatens the emotional starvation of the people. The pent-up emotions of the people make them uncomfortable and miserable. They need to "express themselves," and they cannot do this when they spend their lives calculating for power and goods. And this is where "the artist," rather the esthete, comes in. It is his task to give men an emotional outlet without disturbing their career of acquisition. He must enable men to express the whole range of emotions without affecting the manner of their lives or the course of their actions. Whatever he does, he must not impede the progress of civilization, and he must not combat the lusts it generates. His "art" must not call for discipline and intelligence. Its function is not to encourage humility and love. Such art is expected to excite the emotions, but it is no longer expected to purify them. Its clarifications must be free from ambiguity. Art may be difficult or simple, realistic or romantic, naturalistic or geometrical, or anything, so long as it is not ambiguous. Heaven knows, existence is ambiguous enough. In art, one must know how one feels, and the stronger one feels about it, the better. It may be pretty or ugly, funny or sad, about good or evil. But, in any case, we must know where we are. We must know what the thing "means"; or at least it must mean something we would know if we were clever enough. Knowing what it means, we must feel one way or another because of it. Art is become the means of escape from the ambiguity of existence. Whatever such "art" does to us, it cannot and does not purify our lust. On the contrary, as a source of sentimentalism, it deepens the corruption of the civilized soul and quickens the pace of death. Decadent art is one which has lost the vision of the ambiguity of existence. Its appearance means that lust has become unmanageable and will soon destroy soul and civilization alike.

Although culture is an antidote to lust, we find lust decomposing it continually into mere thought and mere emotion, and nullifying its power to purify the soul. The more advanced a civilization, that is, the more power there is in a society, the more effete and futile its culture tends to become. In our industrial civilization, the authentic artist is alienated from the common life of the people, and the market is taken over by a host of counterfeiters who have even forgotten what it was they have copied and cheapened. The difficulty is deeper than commercialism. Even rebellious art does not guarantee that we shall have the true article. The evil in our culture today is that the philosopher and the artist themselves have succumbed to the despair of the "modern man." They also have declared themselves innocent. They have disavowed guilt, and refused to subject it to philosophical and artistic criticism. Since the ambiguity of existence is apprehended in the conjunction of despair and guilt, they are no longer taken seriously, either by themselves or by their public, as educators toward "the good life." Culture has been severed from existence and ceases to act as the cathartic without which there is no antidote to lust and no prospect for an intelligent and good existence.

The proverbial tendency of the cultured to think or feel in one way, and to live in quite another, is no accident. Culture is inspired by existence, but the preoccupation of the cultured with ideas and emotions is a constant temptation to dissociate experience from existence. This dissociation is accompanied by a disavowal of guilt; and without a serious view of guilt, we cannot live out the truth of our ambiguous existence. There is no such thing as culture without a creative awareness of guilt. The artist or philosopher who is not serious about guilt moves away from under the shadow which is the source of the light that is in him. When the philosopher ignores guilt, his dialectic becomes abstract and fatuous. When the artist does similarly, he becomes incapable of expressing that mysterious light without which there is no beauty. A philosopher who is not concerned with guilt may produce a metaphysic which takes care of everything under the sun; but he cannot include man in it. An esthete, an artist who cannot respond creatively to guilt, may paint inane madonnas and pretty cherubs, but he cannot for the life of him, paint the *portrait of a man.* A composer with the same blindness may produce clever and exciting music. But he has "nothing to say." Thus it is in every aspect of culture. Where guilt is repudiated and ignored, culture is divorced from life, and degenerates into sophistry and esthetics. A degenerate culture, one which no longer confronts us with our humanity or ambiguous existence, indicates a dehumanization which is death.

Culture is an expression of humanity. Humanity, with its twin concerns of duty and destiny, is prior to culture. It is the source of culture, and the light which is the glory of culture. Hence, humanity cannot be identified either with wisdom or with art. It consists in faith which is both our hope for life and our despair with it, both the presupposition of our guilt and our hope for deliverance from its power. Faith is our existence in relation which makes our despair guilty. It is our existence in unrelation which makes our guilt desperate. Faith is our ambiguous existence in relation to God and in a negative relation to the void. On the other hand, culture is the expression of our existence in thought and sensibility. It is neither self-constituating nor self-maintaining. It draws its boundless energies from faith which endows its works with their characteristic "beauty," or "truth." Hence it is that without faith culture is corrupted into sophistic show and esthetic sham.

Our faith is the primary apprehension of the ambiguity of human existence, expressed in symbols which are embedded in our history. In Christendom, the language of faith is the language of the Christian faith as found in the historic creeds of the Church. Every faith other than the Christian, whether imported or invented, fails to express our particular awareness of the ambiguity of our existence. We may think it is the best we can do, but it is not good enough to cover our case. There are faiths esoteric, faiths scientific, faiths humanistic. But they have failed to sustain our culture. Capitalism, fascism, communism have shaken the foundations of the world, but their combined effect has been and still is demonic, inflaming our lusts and goading us to evil. Present-day nationalism, spread all over the earth like wildfire, is a fury rather than a faith. On the other hand, idealism, eutopeanism, evolutionism, and the like, have become either irrelevant, or fatuous, or both. We have found no substitute for the Christian faith; and we shall not find any. The soul of the Western man was formed by the Christian faith, and this faith alone can nourish and sustain it. Our science and civilization presuppose an attitude towards truth whose ultimate ground is the Christian doctrine of creation. Justice among us is rooted in a sense of humanity derived from the scriptural doctrines of the worth, dignity, and destiny of man. Our sense of beauty itself belongs to our soul as formed by the "mysteries" of the Christian faith. Our families, our economic and political institutions, our schools and churches, even our manners, are unintelligible in their origins and development, apart from the Christian faith. We have no choice between the Christian faith and another, any more than we have a choice between being ourselves and being someone else. It is the fate of Christendom either to exist by the Christian faith or not to exist. This is why a non-Christian Christendom is now engaged in a life and death struggle. Our very existence depends upon a revival of the Christian faith among us.

5. *THE AMBIGUITY OF THE CHRISTIAN FAITH*

The difficulties in the way of such a revival are both theoretical and practical. The first type of difficulty has to do with a radical misinterpretation of the Christian faith as a set of literal symbols. Both belief and unbelief in our time are based upon this error. The Christian faith has become ineffective as the source of culture, and our culture itself is in peril of dissolution, because of the disastrous notion that Christian doctrines denote unambiguous objects. Believers know the thing they believe, the unbelievers know that there is no such thing. An astonishing thing has happened among us. The Christian faith, the source of this faith in us, has itself become unambiguous.

The language of the Christian faith—God, revelation, sin, Christ, forgiveness, etc.—has become a jumble of literal symbols. Believers and unbelievers alike act as though these words referred to well known objects which either do or do not exist. The only serious question about Christian doctrines has become their credibility. Some believe: others do not believe. But whether believers or unbelievers, men misconstrue both the faith and its symbols.

But the Apostles' Creed, the catholic statement of the Christian faith, is not a set of literal symbols. God, the first article of the Creed, is not an object which we might imagine as we do the object symbolized by "a table." God cannot be imagined because He does not exist as do His handiwork. He has a peculiar essence and exists in a manner peculiar to Himself; and neither His essence nor His existence can be imagined. On the other hand, as the Maker of all things, He exists in relation to them. Having made them, He is other than they are. He exists as they exist, otherwise He could not be thought of as existing in relation to them or as being other than they are. Words such as being and existence, when applied to God as literal symbols, confront us with contradiction which is nonsense. As language about God, they are ambiguous metaphors, symbols derived from "heaven and earth" and applied to their Maker. When images are used as literal symbols of God, it is no longer He that is imagined, but a figment of the imagination: that is, an idol.

"The Father," in the Creed, cannot be taken literally. Father literally means a male who has begotten one or more children. It is superstition to believe that God begot the Son as a man begets a child. "Father" is a person. A person is "flesh and blood," a man. But it is superstition to believe that God is a man. The next word in the Creed, "Almighty," makes anthropomorphism impossible. If God is a father, He is not almighty. If He is almighty (and perfect in wisdom, love, righteousness, etc.), He is not a father. Father as a literal symbol cannot be applied to God without self-contradiction.

The Creed calls God "the Maker of heaven and earth." Heaven and earth here means everything that exists. It includes all beings everywhere. God is the Maker of all beings. There is nothing that He did not make. He did not make something out of something that He did not make. But, we know nothing of such "making." Anything that anybody makes, he makes out of something that he did not make. "The Maker," therefore, is not a literal symbol of God. On the other hand, we cannot dispense with it, except perhaps for a better synonym such as "the Creator." Heaven and earth were not made in the way that anything in them is made. Having been made, they are dependent for their continued existence upon God in a way which is unlike the dependence of one creature upon another. They exist by God's power in a way no being exists by the power of another. God's power whereby they exist is unlike the power of any being as it affects another. God, as the Creed says, is Almighty. But, He is Almighty in a way peculiar to Himself. The might of the creature overwhelms the power of others. The mightier a man is, the more others are reduced in their power. An almighty man would reduce all others into puppets. But God Almighty empowers His creatures with His omnipotence, and His sovereignty is the ground of their freedom. As literal language, all this is nonsense. But as metaphorical language, it is a definitive expression of the ambiguity of existence itself.

Similar tensions appear in every aspect of Christian thought about God. To expose all of these would require an elaborate treatise on Christian theology. A few suggestive examples must suffice in this connection. It is essential to the catholic faith that God is eternal. No one but a heretic will think of God as having begun to exist, or as being fated to die in however a distant future. But, the eternity of God is not an indefinitely prolonged existence after the fashion of a thing in heaven or on earth. God being the Creator of all things, His duration is incomparable to the duration of man or of the things around him. As the Creator, He exists outside of the times which circumscribe the several existences of His creatures. On the other hand, since all things are created and exist in temporal relations one to another, God's activity is temporal and so is His existence. It follows that God must be thought of as once temporal and non-temporal. Therefore, "eternity" is a metaphorical and not a literal symbol as applied to God's existence.

The same is true of God's infinity. God the Creator is not infinite as heaven and earth might be infinite. All things exist spatially, but God is not "in space." The question of the finitude or the "infinity of the worlds" is not relevant to the manner of God's infinity. God is infinite as the Creator of the universe. On the other hand, since God has created all things in space and sustains them with His omnipresent power, God and space cannot be severed one from the other; and God is everywhere in His creation. But still, as the Creator, He is other than the world. Hence, He is finite as apposite to the world. But, He is not apposite to the world as one thing is apposite to another. Therefore He is not finite as anything is finite. He is infinite . . . "The infinite" as a literal symbol is inapplicable to God. But as a metaphor it is indispensable.

The outstanding double-doctrine in Christianity is that

Jesus Christ is both God and man. The creature's power, even though sustained by God, is no match for the power of sin and death. Hence, it is the power of the Creator as against the power of the creature that overwhelms sin with righteousness and death with life; and it is this power with which Jesus Christ was endowed. Moreover, God did not endow Christ with His omnipotence, and sit back, as it were, idly watching Christ from afar off. "God was in Christ, reconciling the world to Himself." The Son of God, or the Word of God, or God the Son, became incarnate; but in so doing, He was neither separated from God the Father and God the Spirit, nor confined by His humanity . . . On the other hand, Jesus Christ was a man, "in all things like unto us, but without sin." It is intolerable heresy to think of Him as man in body but God in mind. It was by His faith and obedience, by His love to God and His fellowman as required by the "Great Commandment," that He wrought His works of mercy and power. By the same obedience, His cross became a "propitiation" for our sins. It was a human faith, with consequent love and obedience, that found favor with God and reconciled men with God. The doctrine of Christ is ambiguity itself.

This same ambiguity pervades the doctrine of the Christian man. The Christian man is a "new creature." "I believe . . . in the forgiveness of sins." Sin has been replaced by a new righteousness and death by a new life. A new faith, a new hope, a new love, have entered into human life, and all things are made new. We have passed from darkness into light, and by faith everything appears in a new light. The old despair having been removed, sin and death have lost their power over us. Our sins having been forgiven, we no longer live and die in despair. Death having been overwhelmed, we are free from the powers of sin and despair alike. We no longer live in the misery of those dying, but we live or die in the joy of the hope of "the resurrection of the body and the life everlasting." Such is the new life we have in Christ Jesus and to the glory of God . . .

On the other hand, any man who says he is without sin is a liar. The alternative to the pretended innocence of the desperate is not the pretended righteousness of the pharisaical believer. Christianity is not new delusions for the old. "Thou shalt love the Lord thy God with all thy heart, with all thy soul, and with all thy strength; and thy neighbor as thyself." "Whosoever will come after me, let him deny himself, and take up his cross, and follow me." Who can say that he obeys the Great Commandment or that, which is the same thing for the Christian, he has denied himself, and taken up his cross, and followed Jesus? If a man cannot say this, how then is he without sin? If he is not without sin, how then does he know that the power of sin in him is broken and that he has passed from death to life? If sin still has power over him, so does death. His complacency is a poor antidote to the despair and guilt in him, and since he lives under the false light of his own righteousness, lust in him is all the more virulent and unresisted. The man who is not serious when he prays, "Forgive us our debts as we forgive our debtors," knows neither faith nor righteousness. The man who does not say with the Apostle Paul, "We ourselves, who are the first fruits of the Spirit, groan inwardly as we wait for adoption as sons, the redemption of our bodies," knows neither Christian hope nor Christian joy. . . . The terminology of the Christian life—faith, righeousness, hope, love, joy, etc.—is metaphorical and not literal.

The language of the Christian faith is evoked by the ambiguity of existence as revealed by God in Christ Jesus. Its astonishing clarifications or doctrines are so many confirmations of this ambiguity and its primary expressions in the human soul.

No one truly believes as a Christian who does not discern mystery of human existence as unfolded by the doctrines of the Faith. Literalism, dogmatism, pretension to God's knowledge of truth are perversions of faith and doctrine alike. They are denials of the ambiguity of existence and of the ambiguities which permeate the life of man. They constitute a refusal to exist by faith or to live by the truth of our humanity. The dogmatist has already removed himself from under the shadow and from the refreshing influences which emanate from it. Whether he be a believer or an unbeliever, he has lost that humility which is the chief adornment of man. He may often think humbly, and he may feel humble. But he no longer exists in humility, or as a man.

6. THE PROBLEM OF JUSTICE

Christianity is a mode of existence before it is thought and feeling. Thought and feeling arise from existence, but they may be pursued apart from existence. The philosopher may become lost in the ambiguities of his thought and the artist in the ambiguities of his experience. But the Christian is one who exists in ambiguity as evoked by doctrines of the Faith. The Apostles' Creed is the primary proclamation of the ambiguity of existence and the call to exist in that ambiguity. The Faith, with all the riches of its ambiguous language, calls upon us not only to think, or to feel, but to live out our existence. It addresses itself directly to the facts of guilt and despair, not as matters of mere idea or feeling, but as problems of existence itself. To be a Christian is to forswear both the "academic" and the "esthetic," since the former separates thought from existence, and the latter separates sensibility from love. It is to live the true and the beautiful, and thus to do that which is good. This is why Christianity has its own language, which is neither comprehensible nor credible except in the practice of faith, wherein whether we think, or feel, or do, we do it seriously, that is, in fulfilment of our destiny as persons.

The practical impediment to Christianity is the dissociation of the problem of justice from our responsibility for our destiny. Justice is not merely a "giving every man his due" as he seeks some apparent good. A man's "right" to pursue a good is inseparable from his relation to an ambiguous destiny. One cannot do "the right thing by a fellowman" without regard to humanity or to our common life under the shadow of anticipated nonbeing. One cannot exercise "justice" from a position of security, and thus subordinate the right to the good. The constant temptation in human relations is to make certain, before all, of one's power to maintain one's hold upon one's present advantage in a given social order, and to insure oneself toward both its continuance and its increase. Thus justice becomes a fulfilment of obligations whose primary tendency is to further one's own interests. In any case, the pursuit of justice is not allowed to jeopardize the good life as dictated by self-love. It becomes a matter of mutuality in the enjoyment of power and goods, and not a working out of a common destiny.

But, justice which makes it unnecessary to choose between right and apparent good is not justice. One cannot be just except as one "counts the cost" of justice in terms of peril to one's power and security. Justice is to prefer humanity to one's rights under a social contract. It is to expose oneself to loss for the sake of doing justly towards men and women whose good is inseparable from their destiny. It is to love one's neighbor as oneself: that is, to be bound to one's fellowmen in a common fulfilment of duty which shall fulfil the destiny of every person in a given community. To be just is to exist with proper regard for integrity in the pursuit of the transcendent good. It is to pursue a common good as the bearer of that good which is a matter of destiny for oneself and for one's neighbor. In short, in a matter of justice, duty and destiny are so bound together that to do one's duty is to work out one's destiny.

There is no greater impediment to faith than the disassociation of justice from love. The Christian faith cannot be taken seriously where "Thou shalt love thy neighbor as thyself" is not acknowleged as law and matter for the exercise of justice. If a man is not responsible to love his neighbor as himself, he is already more or less just and needs no radical justification as offered by "The Gospel of Jesus Christ." Faith is inseparable from guilt, but guilt is unacknowledged unless one exist by "the law of love." Jesus Christ came bringing forgiveness to sinners.

Unless disobedience to the essence of the law, "Thou shalt love thy neighbor as thyself," be guilty and a source of despair, Christianity is absurd. This is why even while Christianity has become incredible, it has also become superfluous. Men who need not love their neighbor as themselves have also no need for the Gospel of forgiveness in Christ Jesus.

But, it is not clear that we do not need to be justified. If this were the case, we would not be continually engaged in justifying ourselves. Why must every one plead innocence with regard to the evils among us? The earth is filled up with misery: "good measure, pressed down, and shaken together, and running over." And yet, every man is "a decent fellow." He never does evil but justly or usually through ignorance. The good he has failed to do he was not responsible to do and the evil he did was wholly unintended. When he quarrels with his neighbor, it is the neighbor's fault. When the community is torn with conflict, it is due to someone else's guilt. If he and his wife, or partner, or colleague, do not "get along," it is because the latter is wilful and selfish and stupid. He is in general and essentially good. He is consistently just toward his fellowmen. In short, he is a man of integrity—even though he does not love his neighbor as himself. But, every one knows that he is guilty, and his guilt is rooted in that he will not love his neighbor as himself.

We have to face the fact that our society is infested with lust. The lust in men is inflamed by guilt. Their guilt is in their inhumanity, their injustice in not loving their neighbor as themselves. Their guilt is the poison in our common life. Self-justification without obedience to the Great Commandment is not only futile but also destructive of society. Hence "the forgiveness of sins" is the indispensable condition of justice.

We are inevitably Christians. Justice for us has been defined and made necessary by the Christian gospel. We owe our humanity to this same gospel. This humanity we cannot escape. We can either enjoy it through faith, or turn it into a curse through our guilt and despair.

7. *ANTIDOTE TO LUST*

We are quite evidently baffled by the lusts raging in our society. The primary intention of this book has been to offer a radical and illuminating analysis of lust as generated by the corruption of love. We have found the sources of this corruption in despair and guilt, and in the temptations to escape our ambiguous existence through the pursuit of power in several forms. In case our analysis has been correct, it stands to reason that the only radical antidote to lust is love for our fellowmen as human beings. But such love is radically different from the pleasure we have in pursuing or enjoying goods, or in certain human beings as against others. It is not to be identified with good will, sympathy, altruism, or any simple principle of action. The essence of love is a working awareness of oneself and others as "flesh and blood," as beings whose fate it is to live in "the valley of the shadow of death," as "intelligent creation" who exists from day to day in the light of an ambiguous destiny. Since this light reveals our guilt as well as despair, love is inspired by awareness of a common guilt and a serious view of its meaning for human destiny. Critical intelligence applied to guilt and despair, confronts us with the ambiguity of our existence and the necessity of continued intellectual effort toward discerning the ambiguities in our daily conduct toward our fellowmen. Thus we become impressed with the need for continued attention to individual human beings and to the lights and shadows in our ambiguous relations to them. We are constrained to discriminate, to clarify, to qualify and to forgive while we judge. Thus we attain a new understanding of humility, of both justice and kindness. Thus, in short, we exist as human beings.

What this age needs above all else is a new appreciation of "what it takes" to be a human being and to act as one in relation to one's neighbor. The peculiar tragedy of our time is the failure to have a sense for the special intelligence which is required for existing as human beings and the consequent failure to apply ourselves to the quest of wisdom. Science has replaced wisdom. Hence, we have become infernally clever with things and abysmally stupid with people. We can understand and deal with machines, but we can neither understand nor deal with ourselves and our fellowmen. Alas, we are hardly aware that it takes a peculiar intelligence to know and deal with the soul of man: that a man who would be just to his neighbor needs wisdom as well as good will. We work prodigiously at technical improvements which shall multiply the goods we might enjoy. But we have neither head, nor heart, nor hands, which shall enable us to "do justly, to love mercy, and to walk humbly with our God." All serious business today is technical. Human life itself has become a department of technology. Thus our civilization is turned into a lopsided monstrosity which is always on the verge of tumbling down.

There is no simple, quick, remedy for this situation. It is possible that the original good sense of mankind, in spite of its present ineffectiveness, being still operative among "the people," will, at the last, snatch our civilization from the jaws of predicted Destruction. But we cannot rest comfortable with this possibility. It is in fact extremely probable that unless this good sense or humanity realizes a new effectiveness, it is incapable of performing the miracle we, with so little hope, expect of it. "Faith in man" today is a bit of perilous gambling.

There is not a phase of human enterprise that might be neglected. We cannot do without the scientific method, technical skill, and the vast amount of factual knowledge which has been made available by competent men, including doctors, psychologists and sociologists. We are in very great need of understanding and taking seriously the pervasive and formative influences emanating from our machine-made civilization. We need to take to heart the meaning of "city culture," of cars, the radio, the press, etc., for our existence today. We need to know our economic and political institutions, and to acquire a working aptitude for distinguishing between fact and "ideology" with regard to social relations. We need to clarify our own actual position in the social orders and disorders of our time, and to assume responsibility for justice and the common good.

Still, when knowledge fails to yield proportionate success in human affairs, when even zealous good will fails to achieve good purpose, when utmost exertions leave us dangling at the edge of the precipice—then it is time to think in a new direction. Then it is time to wonder if the difficulty be not in ourselves, as well as around us. Unlikely as it seems at first, we ourselves may be the problem of problems: we ourselves, not as concerned with this good or that, but as we exist in relation to our destiny. It is most likely that we have ignored a truth available through, not science, but self-criticism and self-awareness which only philosophy and art respectively can give. Perhaps, and if our analysis has been correct, certainly, there is a species of truth, indispensable for understanding human affairs, which can be had only through the wisdom and sensibility derived not from science but from culture. Our society cannot exist without both science and wisdom, without civilization and culture. It is, therefore, a very serious matter that there be a new comprehension of culture as the soul of a human community, that philosophy and art become serious public concern. To such an end, it is necessary that culture once again reveal the ambiguities of human existence and promote a living awareness of these ambiguities among us. Philosophy once again must become the quest for wisdom, and art must become a quest for beauty. The philosopher and the artist must "find themselves" in assuming their responsibility to lure men to the shadow whose gloom is light. They must encourage the contemplation of truth and beauty as reflected by the human soul. They must inspire wonder and humility without which men turn into monsters and devour one another. Culture is indispensable for the good health of society.

Our situation makes it clear that neither wisdom nor the sense of beauty is self-maintaining, especially in our society where the temptation to live by power is overwhelming. We must face the fact that philosophy becomes academic and art loses its cathartic virtue. Moreover, the wisdom and sensibility among the people are no match for the lusts permeated through our common life. Humanity must continually draw upon faith, and faith must be energized by hope. The despair and guilt in the modern soul constitute a chemical so potent as to make the denaturement of love inevitable. Neither the philosopher, nor the artist, nor any man, can escape the corrosive influence of atheism. Without faith, love is enervated and left limp and impotent. Faith, therefore, is indispensable for love as love is for a good society.

It is most disturbing to realize that our culture cannot endure without faith whose authentic language in Christendom is the Apostles' Creed. How then can there be hope for "this faithless generation"? There is too much infatuation with machines and goods; too much misunderstanding of the Christian faith, within the churches as well as outside them; too much unacknowledged despair and too little conviction of guilt; too much power, tempting men and nations to lord it one over another. Besides, religion itself is much too uncritical and uncreative. If our future depends upon our faith, our case appears hopeless. Still, we do not know our future as settled. The Christian faith has deep roots in our history and culture. We may think as atheists and feel as esthetes, but we do not and cannot exist without faith. We still care about justice, freedom, order, self-respect, common weal, which are fruits of faith. There are many among us who hate the misuse of men and the lording of one man over another. There are humble men and women everywhere who have not lost their humanity and might "in a pinch" decide to live as human beings rather than die as fiends. And so long as they exist, they exist ambiguously; they exist by faith, and they may act wisely. In a society formed by the Christian faith, there are hidden as well as visible powers making for wisdom. The boundless energy which the Christian faith has released in the world is not spent. To an alarming extent it has become lustful, and is driving us toward ruin. But still, signs of its beneficent working are everywhere, and it is in truth possible that it will become effective toward a new life of wisdom and justice among us.

However, the probabilities of our situation are grim. The total tendency of our work is toward evil. The love among us is not sufficient to halt the rush of our lusts toward the calamities which are causing us to despair in our hearts. An energetic catharsis in our souls has become a necessity for our very existence. Such a catharsis can come only from a faith as inspired and empowered by the Christian Gospel. A new understanding of our existence through the Christian faith, a new sense of our common humanity, a new wisdom, a new humility, a new charity, in short, a radical transformation of our souls, is our only rational hope for a destiny which shall be life and not death to us.

Our lust itself, with its misery and miserable effects, is witness against us that we cannot exist apart from God. The loss of humanity through lust is sufficient evidence of the guilt of despair which turns the love of life into a lust for power. There is no antidote to lust, no recovery of our humanity, except through existence in the truth of our guilt and despair. If we own our guilt, we shall be saved of our despair. If we own our despair, our guilt shall be removed. We know our guilt through the forgiveness of God in Christ, and our despair through the hope of eternal life in the same Christ whom "God raised from the dead." The same light which reveals the death of our souls through lust, reveals also our life "hid with God in Christ." This light is the source of our humanity or ambiguous existence, of our civilization and culture, of our very lives as people who must work out our destiny according to "the law of love." We shall escape the perils before us, and see life and good, as our lust is purified by this same beneficent light which shall be to us for a sane and joyful existence—from God and to God.

INDEX

Absolute, The, 47f.
Ambiguity, of the Christian Faith, 106f., 160f.; and culture, 150f.; of existence, 145f.; of the machine, 16f.; of motives, 33f., 147.
Angels, 55, 111f.
Anxiety, 90f.
Art, 152f., 170.
Atheism, 121f., 144f.

Beauty, 152f.
Being and nonbeing, 50n., 55f., 60f., 68, 75f., 81, 97f.

Callousness, 92, 136f.
Capitalism, 21.
Christian Faith, The, 104f., 121f., 143, 159f., 163f., 171.
Civilization, 13, 148f., 154.
Communism, 22.
Complacency, 30.
Culture, 54, 150f., 158f., 169.

Death, 51n., 61, 63, 97f., 106f., 129f.
Dehumanization, 35f., 61f.
Despair, 67f., 81, 101f., 131; and Christianity, 106f.; and guilt, 96f., 143f.; and love, 138f.; among machines, 123f.; the new, 107f., 120f.

Ego, 83, 135.

Emotions, 66f., 156f.
Enmity, 71, 99f.
Envy, 28f., 70f.
Epistemology, 114f.
Eternal life, 60f., 144f.
Existence, 50n.f., 57, 60, 74f., 97f., 143f., 149, 153f.

Faith, 143f., 145, 167, 171; and ambiguity, 159.
Freedom, 3, Chap. 4.

Gluttony, 69.
God, 104f., 112, 121f., 160f., 172; and guilt, 87f., 100.
Goods, 7f., 70f.
Greed, 8f., 57f.
Guilt, Chap. 5; and despair, 144f.; and the new innocence, 87f., 92f., 100f., 157; not social invention, 91f.

Humanitarianism, 34f., 64, 135f.

Idealism, 116.
Imagination, 153f.
Indifference, 35f., 134f.
Infinity, of goods, 8f., 60f.; of God, 162; of space, 108f., 132, 144f.

Justice, 165f.
Justification, 166f.
Jesus Christ, 162f.

Lifetime, 48f., 55f., 58f., 140f.
Loneliness, in society, 26, 36f., 131f.; in the world, 108f.
Love, 82f., 138, 142, 166f.
Love of life, 57, 61f., 82f., 123f., 140f.
Lust for Freedom, Chap. 4.
Lust for Power, defined, 38f.; and guilt, 101f.; and machines, 13f., 24f.; sources, 6f., 28f., 38f., 59f., 73f.; unnatural, 3f., 40.

Machines, effects upon human life, 8f., 13f., 40, 61f., 77f., 88f.; and despair, 123f.; and ethics, 88f.; and lust, 13f., 24f., 40; the new bondage, 16f.; and social organization, 27f., 31f.; as spirit, 17f.
Man, 42f., 47f., 61f., 97f., 104f., 108f., 141f.
Materialism, 61f., 115.

Nature, Life in, 12, 24, 33f.
Nihilism, 104f.

Person, 52f., 62f., 95f., 145f.
Philosophy, and ambiguity, 150f.; a human enterprise, 113f.
Power, 20, 24f., 27f., 71f.
Pragmatism, 117.
Pride, 32f., 67f.
Psychology, 5f.

Reason, 135, 148f. See also under Unreason and Wisdom.
Romanticism, 118f.

Science, 126f., 148f., 169.
Security, 2, 39f., 102.
Self, The, 79f., 115f.
Self-justification, 102f., 167.
Selfishness, 66, 135f.
Self-hatred, 102, 135f.
Self-love, 135.
Self-pity, 91, 101, 135f.
Seriousness, 145f.
Sex, 69f.
Sin, 106f., 163f.
Skepticism, 117.
Social conflict, 21.
Space, 108f., 132, 144f.
Spirits, old and new, 16f.; man's neighbors, 111f.
Superiority, 31.

Time, 48f., 50f., 55f.
Tragedy, 105.

Unreason, 42f., 64f.

Vices not natural, 64f.
Void, The, 111f., 144f.

Western man, The, 110f., 132f., 144f.
Wisdom, 141, 149f., 168.